The Open University

MST121
Using Mathematics

Chapter A2

Lines and circles

About this course

This course, MST121 *Using Mathematics*, and the courses MU120 *Open Mathematics* and MS221 *Exploring Mathematics* provide a flexible means of entry to university-level mathematics. Further details may be obtained from the address below.

MST121 uses the software program Mathcad (MathSoft, Inc.) and other software to investigate mathematical and statistical concepts and as a tool in problem solving. This software is provided as part of the course.

This publication forms part of an Open University course. Details of this and other Open University courses can be obtained from the Student Registration and Enquiry Service, The Open University, PO Box 197, Milton Keynes MK7 6BJ, United Kingdom: tel. +44 (0)845 300 6090, email general-enquiries@open.ac.uk

Alternatively, you may visit the Open University website at http://www.open.ac.uk where you can learn more about the wide range of courses and packs offered at all levels by The Open University.

To purchase a selection of Open University course materials visit http://www.ouw.co.uk, or contact Open University Worldwide, Walton Hall, Milton Keynes MK7 6AA, United Kingdom, for a brochure: tel. +44 (0)1908 858793, fax +44 (0)1908 858787, email ouw-customer-services@open.ac.uk

The Open University, Walton Hall, Milton Keynes, MK7 6AA.

First published 1997. Second edition 2001. Third edition 2008. Reprinted 2008.

Edited, designed and typeset by The Open University, using the Open University TEX System.

Printed in the United Kingdom by Cambrian Printers, Aberystwyth.

ISBN 978 0 7492 2938 2

3.2

Contents

Study guide

This chapter contains five sections, which are intended to be studied consecutively, and an appendix. Sections 1, 2 and 4 are of average length, and the other two are relatively short. The Appendix can be read, for interest, at any time after Section 3.

You will need access to your DVD player at the start of Subsection 2.1. However, if this is not convenient, then continue with the text and view the video when this becomes feasible. You will need access to your computer and Computer Book A in order to study Section 5.

Although this chapter may look long, it should require no more than average study time since some of the ideas included in the *Revision Pack* are revisited – in particular, the topics of coordinates and lines, and trigonometry.

The division of your time for the chapter might be as follows.

Study session 1: Section 1.

Study session 2: Section 2.

Study session 3: Section 3.

Study session 4: Section 4 and Section 5.

Sections 4 and 5 could be split into two study sessions.

The organisation of your time within each study session is likely to depend on your experience and confidence in working with algebraic expressions.

In addition to the topics mentioned in the third paragraph above, before studying this chapter you should also be familiar with the following topics from the *Revision Pack*:

- ◇ Pythagoras' Theorem;
- ◇ radian measure for angles;
- ◇ similar triangles.

> The optional Video Band A(iv) *Algebra workout – Quadratic equations* could be viewed at any stage during your study of this chapter.

Introduction

Lines and circles are used extensively as models of objects within the real world and of paths which describe the motions of objects. Approximate occurrences of these geometrical shapes occur in nature, and they have been used as a basis for many human artefacts, both ancient and modern.

This chapter concentrates mainly upon the mathematical description and properties of lines and circles. While it is natural to think of them in geometric terms, it is also possible to describe them algebraically. In fact, it is one of the triumphs of mathematics to have created the link between geometry and algebra. Geometry relies more upon our visual sense, whereas algebra can be regarded as a means of coding visual items in a form that appears more abstract but renders calculations easier. In a sense, algebra can be used to model geometric statements. It is often the case that a geometric problem may be translated into algebraic terms, solved using algebraic manipulation, and then interpreted once more geometrically. The study here of lines and circles illustrates this process.

You will also see the topic of *trigonometry* introduced here, since it is connected both with circles and with triangles (which are geometric objects made up from segments of lines). It offers further scope to describe and interpret a geometric view of the world in algebraic terms.

Section 1 shows how lines can be represented by algebraic equations, via a statement of the geometrical restriction which in effect defines what a (straight) line is. You will then see how the point at the intersection of a pair of lines may be calculated by solving simultaneously the equations which represent the lines.

In mathematics, the word *line* usually means *straight* line.

Section 2 seeks to carry out a similar programme for circles, which relies upon the use of *Pythagoras' Theorem.* An important algebraic procedure, known as *completing the square* for an expression of the form $x^2 + 2px$, is explained and applied here.

In Section 3, the trigonometric quantities *sine* and *cosine* are introduced in terms of the coordinates of points on a circle. Their expression as ratios within a right-angled triangle, with which you may be more familiar, is also made apparent.

The ideas in the first three sections are developed in the introduction of *parametric equations* in Section 4. For an object travelling in space, a single equation that relates the spatial coordinates of the object can describe its overall trajectory. On the other hand, parametric equations can be used to express each spatial coordinate in terms of the elapsed time, which permits the motion along the trajectory to be described. There is computer work in Section 5 associated with the topics in Section 4.

The Appendix indicates how some of the ideas of the chapter can be applied in triangulation for mapping purposes and in a global positioning system.

1 Lines

This section shows how certain equations describe lines, and demonstrates some practical uses for this algebraic description. Subsection 1.1 introduces the general form which the equation of a line takes, and shows how the appropriate equation may be found in specific cases. It goes on to consider how the equations of two lines can be used to find their intersection point. Subsection 1.2 looks briefly at some modelling applications of this mathematics.

1.1 Equations of lines

Points and coordinates

The adjective *Cartesian* comes from the surname of the famous French mathematician and philosopher René Descartes (1596–1650). He is credited with being the first to realise that curves and surfaces can be studied not just using ideas of shape, but also using the tools of algebra.

As you know, points in the plane may be specified by pairs of coordinates. We generally use a *rectangular* or *Cartesian* coordinate system to do this, in which a pair of straight lines at right angles are chosen as the *x-axis* and *y-axis* of the system. The point of intersection of these axes is called the *origin*, which is usually labelled O and described by the coordinates $(0, 0)$. Each of the x-axis and y-axis is drawn with an arrowhead to indicate a positive direction along it, as shown in Figure 1.1. Each axis can be regarded as a copy of the real number line, with a uniform scale along it. (Usually, the same scale is used for each axis.)

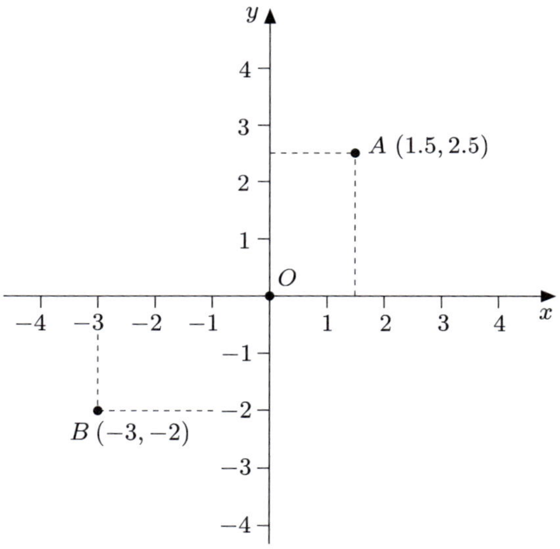

Figure 1.1 Cartesian coordinates

Figure 1.1 shows two points, A and B. The point A has coordinates $(1.5, 2.5)$, because it is reached by moving from O by 1.5 units in the positive x-direction and 2.5 units in the positive y-direction. Similarly, point B has coordinates $(-3, -2)$, because it is reached by moving from O by 3 units in the negative x-direction and 2 units in the negative y-direction.

More generally, a point with coordinates (x, y) is

to the right of the y-axis if $x > 0$,
to the left of the y-axis if $x < 0$,

and

above the x-axis if $y > 0$,
below the x-axis if $y < 0$.

For a point (x, y) on the y-axis itself, we have $x = 0$. Similarly, if (x, y) lies on the x-axis, then $y = 0$.

Lines parallel to the coordinate axes

You probably have a good intuitive sense of what the straightness associated with lines means. One way of putting it is that as you move along a straight line, you maintain the same direction. However, this observation leaves us some way short of being able to describe lines by equations.

The equation of a straight line, or indeed of any curve, specifies the property or condition that is satisfied by the coordinates (x, y) of any point on that line or curve. For example, the two axes of a Cartesian coordinate system are themselves straight lines. All points on the x-axis have the property that their y-coordinate is zero, because to arrive at these points we do not need to move at all in the y-direction. The x-coordinate of such a point depends on how far from the origin the point is, and whether we need to move left ($x < 0$) or right ($x > 0$) from the origin to reach it. Thus the coordinates of all points on the x-axis have the form $(x, 0)$.

The line or curve is sometimes called the *locus* of the equation.

Consequently, we describe the x-axis as the line consisting of all points (x, y) for which $y = 0$. Hence the equation $y = 0$ is an algebraic representation of the x-axis. Similarly, the equation $x = 0$ is an algebraic representation of the y-axis, since the property which distinguishes points on the y-axis is that their x-coordinate is zero; all points here have coordinates of the form $(0, y)$.

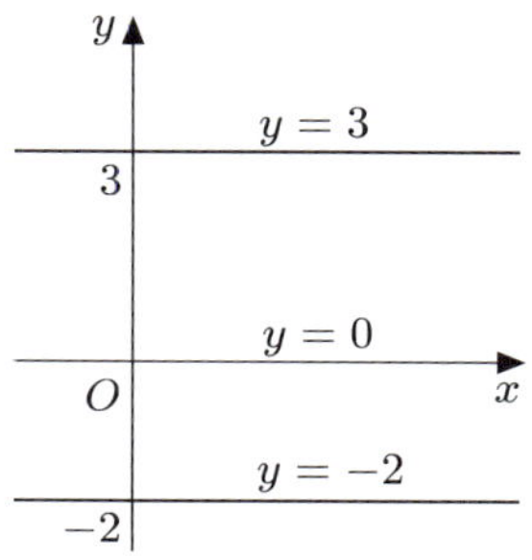

Figure 1.2
Lines parallel to the x-axis

This connection between lines and equations extends to any line which is *parallel* to either the x- or y-axis. Consider, for example, the line which is 3 units vertically above the x-axis. Any point on this line has coordinates of the form $(x, 3)$. We can therefore use the equation $y = 3$ to represent the line. Similarly, the equation $y = -2$ represents the line which is parallel to the x-axis but 2 units vertically below it. The lines $y = 3$ and $y = -2$ are shown in Figure 1.2.

The phrase 'the line $y = 3$' is shorthand for 'the line whose equation is $y = 3$'. Shorthand forms like this are in common use.

In general, any line parallel to the x-axis has an equation of the form $y = c$, where c is a constant. The value of c is positive for a line above the x-axis, and negative for a line below.

Activity 1.1 Parallel to the y-axis

(a) A line is parallel to and 3 units to the left of the y-axis. Write down the equation which represents the line.

(b) Write down the general form of equation for a line parallel to the y-axis. Explain how to distinguish between the two cases in which the line is to the left or to the right of the y-axis.

(c) Sketch each of the lines $x = -3$ and $x = 4$.

Solutions are given on page 53.

As you found in this activity, any line parallel to the y-axis has an equation of the form $x = d$, where d is a constant. It remains now to determine what equations correspond to lines that are not parallel to a coordinate axis.

Equations of lines in general

The shorthand $A(-2, 0)$, for example, means that the point labelled A has coordinates $(-2, 0)$.

Consider first the line which cuts the x-axis at the point $A(-2, 0)$ and the y-axis at the point $B(0, 1)$. This line is shown in Figure 1.3.

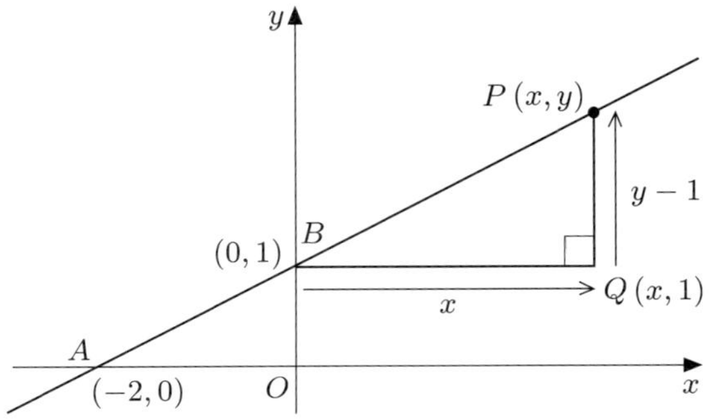

Figure 1.3 P lies on the line through A and B

In the following discussion, $x > 0$ and $y > 1$.

The point P, with coordinates (x, y), is chosen to lie on this line. What algebraic condition on x and y represents the fact that (x, y) lies on the line?

Similar triangles have the same shape.

Let Q be the point on the same vertical line as P and on the same horizontal line as B – see Figure 1.3. Then the straightness of the line ABP means that the triangles ABO and BPQ are *similar* to each other, so that the ratios of lengths of corresponding sides are equal. For example, we have

$$\frac{OB}{AO} = \frac{QP}{BQ}.$$

This leads to the algebraic condition which we seek. The horizontal length AO and vertical length OB are found, from the coordinates of the points $A(-2, 0)$, $B(0, 1)$ and $O(0, 0)$, to be

$$AO = 0 - (-2) = 2 \quad \text{and} \quad OB = 1 - 0 = 1.$$

The point Q has the same x-coordinate as P and the same y-coordinate as B, so its coordinates are $(x, 1)$. It follows that

$$BQ = x - 0 = x \quad \text{and} \quad QP = y - 1.$$

The condition above for the ratios of corresponding sides therefore yields the equation

$$\frac{1}{2} = \frac{y-1}{x}.$$

After multiplying through by x and then making y the subject of the equation, this becomes

In fact, this equation holds for all points (x, y) on the line.

$$y = \tfrac{1}{2}x + 1,$$

which is the equation of the line shown in Figure 1.3. As a check, the pair of values $x = -2$, $y = 0$ satisfies this equation (the point $(-2, 0)$ lies on the line), as does the pair of values $x = 0$, $y = 1$ (the point $(0, 1)$ lies on the line).

It is worth analysing the manner in which this equation was derived, since the approach can be applied more generally. Referring back once more to Figure 1.3, what we did was to equate the ratios OB/AO and QP/BQ, working from a pair of similar triangles. In the first of these ratios, OB is the vertical change from A to B, while AO is the horizontal change from A to B. The second ratio similarly features the vertical change QP and horizontal change BQ between the two points B and P. In fact, whatever pair of points is chosen on the line,

the ratio of vertical to horizontal change between them is the same.

This ratio is a characteristic property of the line itself, called its *slope* or *gradient*.

The slope of the line in Figure 1.3 is $\frac{1}{2}$.

We now consider this idea more generally. Suppose that $A(x_1, y_1)$ and $B(x_2, y_2)$ are any two points on a given line, as shown in Figure 1.4.

Note the use of subscript notation here, with x_1 for 'x-coordinate of first point', x_2 for 'x-coordinate of second point', and so on.

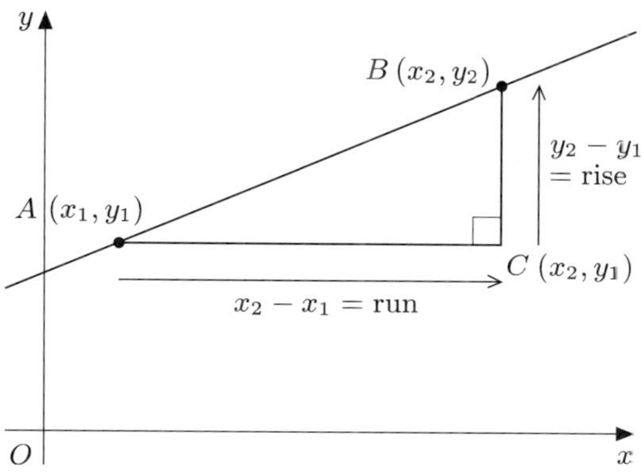

Figure 1.4 Rise and run

Starting from A, we reach B by moving horizontally (in the x-direction) by $x_2 - x_1$ along AC, and vertically (in the y-direction) by $y_2 - y_1$ along CB. We call the vertical change $y_2 - y_1$ the **rise** in moving from A to B, while the horizontal change $x_2 - x_1$ is called the corresponding **run**. As drawn in Figure 1.4, both the rise and the run from A to B are positive quantities, since B is to the right of and above A. If, alternatively, B were below A (so that $y_2 < y_1$), then the rise from A to B would be negative. In fact, the 'rise' in this case would actually describe a fall. If B were to the left of A (so that $x_2 < x_1$), then the run from A to B would be negative.

In these definitions, the order of the points is significant. The rise from B to A has the opposite sign to the rise from A to B.

As was remarked upon in a specific case earlier, the straightness of the line in Figure 1.4 can be described by the observation that, however the two points A and B are chosen on the line, the ratio of the rise to the run from A to B is the same. This ratio is called the **slope** or **gradient** of the line.

This follows from the fact that all right-angled triangles ABC, as in Figure 1.4, which can be drawn with A, B on the line, are similar to one another.

Rise, run and slope

For any pair of points, $A(x_1, y_1)$ and $B(x_2, y_2)$, on a given line, the **rise** from A to B is $y_2 - y_1$ and the **run** from A to B is $x_2 - x_1$. If the run is not zero, then the quantity 'rise ÷ run' (called the **slope** of the line) is independent of the pair of points chosen.

The definition of slope can be summed up in the phrase 'slope equals rise over run'.

Activity 1.2 Two special cases

(a) The statement above excludes the case where the run between the two points is zero (as it must, to avoid the undefined operation of 'division by zero'). What type of straight line leads to a zero run between two points on the line?

(b) What type of line has zero slope?

Solutions are given on page 53.

As you saw in the solution to Activity 1.2(a), every line of the form $x = d$, where d is a constant, has **infinite slope**.

We found the equation for the line shown in Figure 1.3 by equating two expressions for the slope of the line: one in terms of the coordinates of the two known points A and B, which gave the numerical value $\frac{1}{2}$ for the slope, and the other in terms of B and a further general point P whose coordinates (x, y) were unspecified. This procedure generalises as follows.

If $A(x_1, y_1)$ and $B(x_2, y_2)$ are any two points with known coordinates on a given line, then the slope m of the line is given by

$$m = \frac{\text{rise from } A \text{ to } B}{\text{run from } A \text{ to } B} = \frac{y_2 - y_1}{x_2 - x_1}, \tag{1.1}$$

as illustrated in Figure 1.5(a).

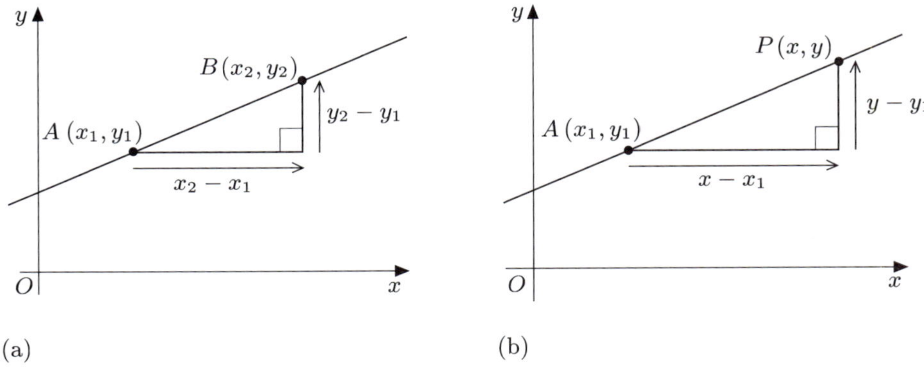

Figure 1.5 Rise and run: particular and general cases

Now let $P(x, y)$ be a general point on the line, as shown in Figure 1.5(b). The slope is expressible once again as

$$m = \frac{\text{rise from } A \text{ to } P}{\text{run from } A \text{ to } P} = \frac{y - y_1}{x - x_1}. \tag{1.2}$$

Equation (1.1) permits calculation of the value of m, given any two points on the line. Equation (1.2) then provides an algebraic connection between the variables x and y, which embodies the condition that the point (x, y) lies on the line. Equation (1.2) can be rearranged as follows:

$$y - y_1 = m(x - x_1); \quad \text{that is,} \quad y = mx + (y_1 - mx_1).$$

Here m, x_1 and y_1 are constants. The equation of a line therefore has the form

$$y = mx + c,$$

where m and c are constants for any particular line.

This covers all cases except that of lines parallel to the y-axis, as considered in Activity 1 2(a).

The symbol m stands for the *slope* of the line. To interpret the symbol c, note that the point $(0, c)$ lies on both the y-axis and on the line $y = mx + c$. Hence c is the value of y where the line $y = mx + c$ cuts the y-axis, which is called the **y-intercept** of the line. Similarly, the value of x where the line cuts the x-axis is called the **x-intercept** of the line. These intercepts are illustrated in Figure 1.6.

The line shown in Figure 1.3 has y-intercept 1 and x-intercept -2.

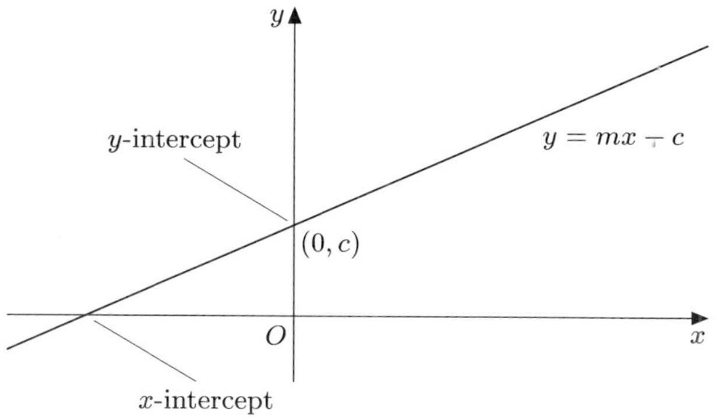

Figure 1.6 Intercepts

The slope m of a line gives an indication of how steep the line is.

If m is zero, then the line is horizontal (parallel to the x-axis).

If m is positive, then the line rises from left to right. The steepness of the line increases for greater values of m. This is illustrated in Figure 1.7(a) for lines through the origin, for which $c = 0$ and the equation of the line becomes $y = mx$.

If m is negative, then the line falls from left to right. The larger the *magnitude* of m, the steeper is the corresponding line (see Figure 1.7(b)).

The **magnitude** of a number a is a if $a \geq 0$, and $-a$ if $a < 0$. For example, the magnitudes of 2 and -2 are both 2.

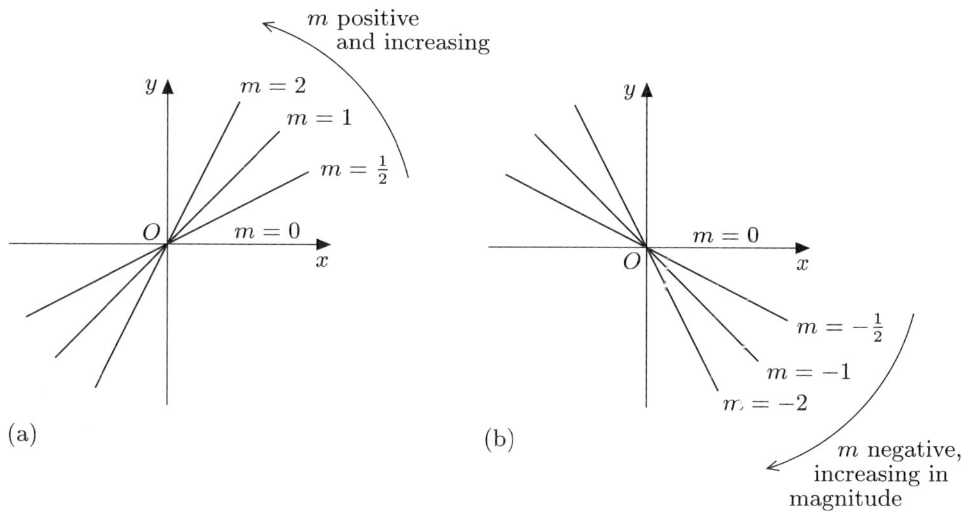

Figure 1.7 Steepness and slope

Activity 1.3 Sketching lines – a reminder

To sketch a line $y = mx + c$, it is sufficient to find two points on the line. It is usually convenient to choose one point to be $(0, c)$. Sketch the line which corresponds to each of the following equations.

(a) $y = \frac{1}{3}x$ (b) $y = -2x$ (c) $y = 2x - 1$ (d) $y = -3x + 1$

Solutions are given on page 53.

Activity 1.3 concerned lines whose equations were given. It is often the case that we need to find the equation of a line, starting from other information about it. The next example shows how to tackle such problems, using the information about the equations of lines obtained so far, which is summarised below.

The equation of a line

Any line which is not parallel to the y-axis has an equation of the form

$$y = mx + c,$$

where m is the slope of the line and c is its y-intercept. The equation can also be expressed as

$$y - y_1 = m(x - x_1),$$

where (x_1, y_1) is any one point on the line. The slope m can be calculated from the formula

$$m = \frac{y_2 - y_1}{x_2 - x_1},$$

where (x_1, y_1) and (x_2, y_2) are two points on the line.

Note that the formula for the slope can equally well be written as

$$m = \frac{y_1 - y_2}{x_1 - x_2},$$

showing that the order in which the two points are taken does not affect the outcome, provided that the order is the same in the denominator as in the numerator.

Example 1.1 Finding equations of lines

(a) Find the equation of the line which has slope 3 and passes through the point $(1, -2)$.

(b) Find the equation of the line which passes through the points $(1, 5)$ and $(4, -7)$.

Solution

(a) Since both the slope of the line and one point on it are given, we may apply the equation $y - y_1 = m(x - x_1)$ in this case, with $m = 3$ and $(x_1, y_1) = (1, -2)$. This gives

$$y - (-2) = 3(x - 1).$$

On multiplying out the brackets and then subtracting 2 from both sides, this becomes

$$y = 3x - 5.$$

As a check, the equation is indeed satisfied by the pair of values $x = 1$ and $y = -2$ (as it must be if the point $(1, -2)$ is to lie on the line as specified).

(b) Here the slope of the line is not given initially, but it can be calculated from the rise and run involved in moving between the given points. From $(1,5)$ to $(4,-7)$, the run is $4-1=3$ and the rise is $-7-5=-12$. Hence the slope m is given by

$$m = \frac{\text{rise}}{\text{run}} = \frac{-12}{3} = -4.$$

Now we can proceed as in part (a), applying the equation $y - y_1 = m(x - x_1)$ with $m = -4$ and *either* $(x_1, y_1) = (1,5)$ *or* $(x_1, y_1) = (4,-7)$. Taking the first possibility, we have

$$y - 5 = -4(x - 1).$$

You may like to check that the second possibility leads to the same equation for the line.

On multiplying out the brackets and then adding 5 to both sides, this becomes

$$y = -4x + 9.$$

As a check, the equation is indeed satisfied by the pair of values $x = 1$ and $y = 5$ (as it must be if the point $(1,5)$ is to lie on the line as specified). Similarly, the point $(4,-7)$ does lie on the line as required, since the equation is satisfied by the pair of values $x = 4$ and $y = -7$.

Activity 1.4 Finding equations of lines

(a) Find the equation of the line which has slope -2 and passes through the point $(5,-3)$.

(b) Find the equation of the line which has x-intercept 3 and y-intercept -6 (that is, the line which passes through the points $(3,0)$ and $(0,-6)$).

Solutions are given on page 53.

Parallel lines

Note that two (distinct) lines are parallel whenever they have the same slope, since they are then 'equally steep'. For example, the line $y = 3x + 2$ is parallel to the line $y = 3x$. The '+2' in the first equation indicates that the first line is a vertical distance 2 units above the second line. Similarly, the line $y = 3x - 1$ is also parallel to the line $y = 3x$, but a vertical distance 1 unit below it. These three lines are shown in Figure 1.8.

Different scales have been used for the axes in Figure 1.8 in order that the figure is not too large. The fact that the lines are parallel is not affected.

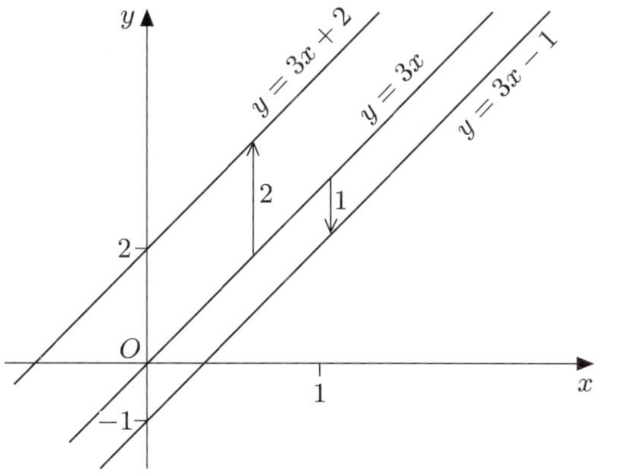

Figure 1.8 Parallel lines

Perpendicular lines

We see next that there is a simple connection between the slopes of two lines which are perpendicular (at right angles to each other). First try the following activity.

Activity 1.5 Perpendicularity in a particular case

Plot the points $A(2, 3)$, $B(1, 1)$ and $C(4, 2)$, using the same scale for each axis, and join AB and AC. Observe that the two line segments AB and AC appear to be perpendicular, and then calculate their slopes.

A solution is given on page 54.

Congruent triangles have the same shape and size.

Now consider the general situation depicted in Figure 1.9, in which the line segment AC has been constructed by rotating a line segment AB through a right angle about A, so that the two triangles marked are *congruent*.

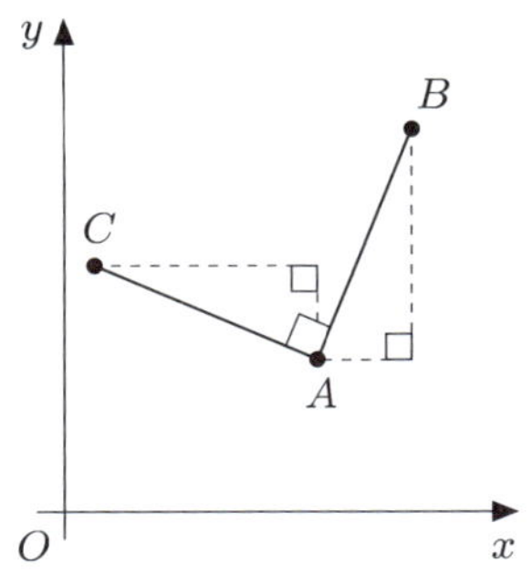

Figure 1.9 Congruent triangles

The phrase 'equal in magnitude' means 'equal except for the possibility that they may be of opposite sign'.

Because these triangles are congruent, the rise from A to B is equal in magnitude to the run from A to C, and the run from A to B is equal in magnitude to the rise from A to C. However, if the rise from A to B is positive (as in Figure 1.9), then the run from A to C is negative, and vice versa, whereas the run from A to B and the rise from A to C always have the same sign. Hence we have

$$\text{slope of } AB = \frac{\text{rise from } A \text{ to } B}{\text{run from } A \text{ to } B} = \frac{-\text{run from } A \text{ to } C}{\text{rise from } A \text{ to } C} = \frac{-1}{\text{slope of } AC}.$$

Note that the particular slopes found in Activity 1.5 satisfy this relationship.

Another way of expressing this is to say that

$$(\text{slope of } AB) \times (\text{slope of } AC) = -1.$$

This calculation depends on the slope of AC not being 0 or infinite, since otherwise the division involved would not make sense.

In general, if two lines are perpendicular (but not parallel to the axes), then the product of their slopes is -1, and vice versa.

A line with slope 0 is horizontal; a line with infinite slope is vertical.

Perpendicularity condition

If two lines are perpendicular, then *either* the product of their slopes is -1 *or* one has slope 0 and the other has infinite slope.

Activity 1.6 Applying the perpendicularity condition

(a) The point A has coordinates $(-1,4)$ and the point B has coordinates $(5,2)$. Find the slope of the line AB.

(b) What is the slope of each line perpendicular to AB?

(c) Find the equation of the line which passes through A and is perpendicular to AB.

Solutions are given on page 54.

Intersection of two lines

You have seen how any line may be represented by an equation of the form $y = mx + c$ or (if parallel to the y-axis) $x = d$, where m, c and d are constants. It was pointed out that two lines which have the same slope m are parallel to each other, and hence never intersect. On the other hand, any two lines with different slopes must intersect at exactly one point. This may be visible if the two lines are plotted on a graph, either by hand or by computer, and from such a plot the position of the intersection point can be estimated.

Two curves *intersect*, or *meet*, if they have a point in common.

The intersection point can also be found algebraically. It lies on both of the lines, which means that its coordinates (x, y) satisfy the equations of *both* lines. The values of these coordinates can therefore be found by solving the two equations *simultaneously*. This is illustrated below.

Example 1.2 Finding points of intersection

Find the point at which the line $y = 2x + 3$ meets the line $y = -4x + 1$.

Solution

The coordinates (x, y) of the point of intersection A satisfy both equations,

$$y = 2x + 3 \quad \text{and} \quad y = -4x + 1.$$

Hence the x-coordinate of A must satisfy the equation

$$2x + 3 = -4x + 1; \quad \text{that is,} \quad 6x = -2,$$

This approach to solving these equations is equivalent to substituting the expression for y from the first equation in the second equation, as discussed in Chapter A0.

whose solution is $x = -\frac{1}{3}$. The y-coordinate of A is then found by substituting this value for x into either of the two original equations. For example, putting $x = -\frac{1}{3}$ into the equation $y = 2x + 3$ gives $y = 2 \times (-\frac{1}{3}) + 3 = \frac{7}{3}$. Hence the point of intersection of the two lines has coordinates $(-\frac{1}{3}, \frac{7}{3})$.

As a check, these coordinates also satisfy the second equation, $y = -4x + 1$, since we have $-4(-\frac{1}{3}) + 1 = \frac{7}{3}$.

Activity 1.7 Finding points of intersection

(a) Find the point at which the line $y = 5x - 7$ intersects the line $y = -3x + 1$, by solving the two equations simultaneously.

(b) Show that it is not possible to find the point at which the line $y = 2x + 3$ meets the line $y = 2x - 3$, and explain why this is so.

Solutions are given on page 54.

1.2 Some applications

We now look briefly at how the mathematics in Subsection 1.1 can be applied in the process of modelling real problems. The topic of mathematical modelling was considered first in Chapter A1, Section 7, where a loose framework to describe it was introduced. This framework encompassed five key stages, and in this subsection we are concerned with aspects of the three middle stages, namely, 'Create the model', 'Do the mathematics' and 'Interpret the results'.

Create model

The variables are said to be *linearly related* in such a case.

The stage of creating the model involves choosing variables, stating assumptions and formulating mathematical relationships between the chosen variables. In Chapter A1 the relationships involved were recurrence systems. Here we are interested in the possibility of formulating *linear* relationships, that is, relationships which would be represented by straight lines if plotted on a graph. You have already seen the algebraic form $y = mx + c$ that such a relationship takes, when the variables are x and y. You need to be able to recognise the linear form also when other symbols are chosen for the variables. It will often be the case that the constants m and c represent something significant in the situation being modelled.

Here the symbols t and s take the places of x and y, respectively. It is usual to denote time by t.

For example, if t represents time in seconds, and s metres is the position of an object relative to some fixed point, then the linear relationship $s = 20t + 100$ gives the position of the object at any time, as indicated in the following table. Here $m = 20$ and $c = 100$.

t	0	1	2	3	...
s	100	120	140	160	...

In the context of motion, 'steady' is often used to mean 'constant'.

The object changes position at a steady velocity of $20\,\mathrm{m\,s^{-1}}$ (metres per second), and is at position $s = 100$ when $t = 0$.

Sometimes within a modelling situation there are *two* linear relationships of interest between the same pair of variables. For example, two objects in steady motion over the same period lead to two distance–time equations that represent straight lines. It might then be a matter of interest to determine where, if at all, the objects will meet each other.

Do mathematics

This corresponds to finding the point of intersection of two straight lines, either by drawing their graphs or by adopting the algebraic approach outlined at the end of Subsection 1.1. This corresponds to the 'Do the mathematics' stage of modelling.

Example 1.3 *Coinciding hands*

The positions of the minute and hour hands of a traditional clock coincide at 12 noon. They next coincide at some time after 1 pm (see Figure 1.10). By following the steps below, find this time.

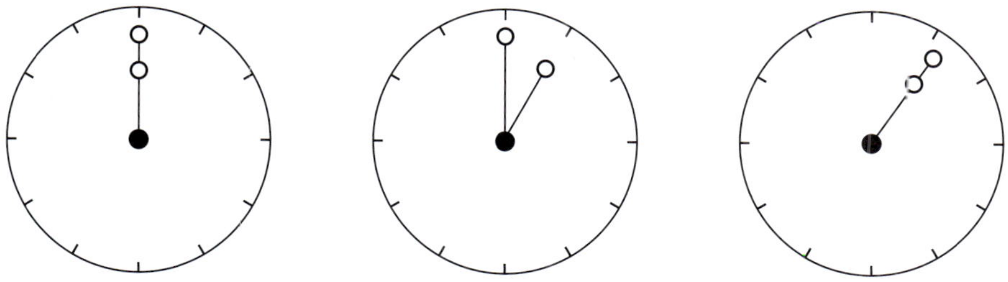

(a) at 12 noon (b) at 1 pm (c) shortly after 1 pm

Figure 1.10 Coinciding hands

(a) Take t to be the time, measured in minutes, after 1 pm. Take θ (> 0) to be the angle in degrees through which a hand has rotated (clockwise!), measured from the '12 o'clock position'. Assume that the hands move steadily, rather than in discrete jumps. Find a linear relationship between t and θ for each of the minute hand and the hour hand.

Unless there is good reason, as here, it is usual to measure anticlockwise rotations by positive angles.

(b) Find the point of intersection of the two lines whose equations were found in part (a).

(c) By interpreting the answer to part (b) appropriately, estimate when the hour and minute hands next coincide on the clock-face after 12 noon.

Solution

(a) There are 360° in a revolution of either hand. The minute hand undergoes one revolution per hour, or $\frac{360}{60} = 6°$ per minute. Hence the slope of the line representing the linear relationship between t and θ in the (t, θ)-plane is 6. Also, since $t = 0$ at 1 pm, we have $\theta = 0$ at $t = 0$. Hence the motion of the minute hand is described by the line with equation

$$\theta = 6t,$$

as shown in Figure 1.11.

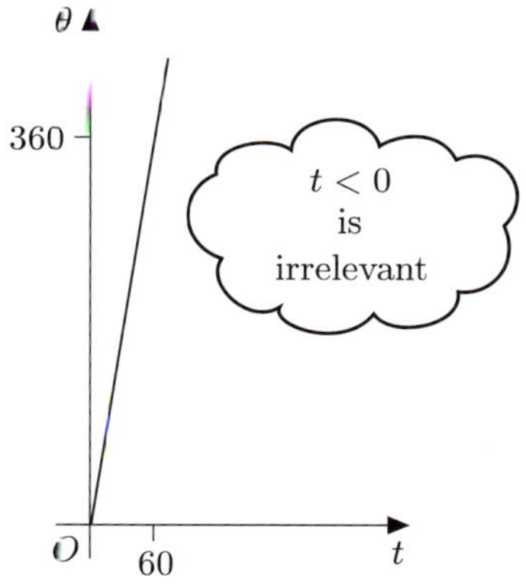

Figure 1.11
The line $\theta = 6t$

Similarly, the hour hand undergoes one revolution every 12 hours, or $\frac{360}{12\times 60} = \frac{1}{2}°$ per minute. At 1 pm ($t = 0$), the hour hand has reached $\theta = 30$, which is $\frac{1}{12}$ of a complete revolution. Its equation therefore takes the form

$$\theta = \tfrac{1}{2}t + c, \quad \text{where } \theta = 30 \text{ when } t = 0.$$

In other words, the line $\theta = \frac{1}{2}t + c$ passes through the point $(t, \theta) = (0, 30)$, so that $c = 30$. The linear relationship for the hour hand is therefore

$$\theta = \tfrac{1}{2}t + 30.$$

(b) The two lines, $\theta = 6t$ and $\theta = \frac{1}{2}t + 30$, meet when

$$6t = \tfrac{1}{2}t + 30; \quad \text{that is,} \quad t = \tfrac{60}{11} \simeq 5.4545.$$

The symbol $\simeq$ is read as 'is approximately equal to'. In this chapter, the approximations are correct to the number of significant figures given.

(c) Since 0.4545 minutes is $60 \times 0.4545 \simeq 27$ seconds, the two hands next coincide (after 12 noon) at about 5 minutes and 27 seconds past 1 pm.

Interpret results

The last part of Example 1.3 corresponds to the 'Interpret the results' stage of modelling.

Activity 1.8 Modelling the motion of trains

A passenger train sets off from Edinburgh Waverley towards London Kings Cross (600 km away) at 7 am. It travels at an average speed of 100 km per hour. On the same day, a freight train starts at 8.30 am from London to Edinburgh, travelling at an average speed of 60 km per hour. In this activity you are asked to estimate the time and position at which the two trains pass one another.

Let d be the distance in kilometres from Edinburgh, and t the time in hours since 7 am. As part of the modelling process, you should assume that the two trains travel steadily at the average speeds given.

(a) Write down an equation which relates d and t for the passenger train.

(b) For the freight train, what are the values of t and d at 8.30 am? Find an equation which relates d and t for the freight train. (Note that the slope of the line involved here will be negative, since during the train's journey d decreases while t increases.)

(c) By sketching the two lines on a graph, estimate when and where the two trains pass one another.

(d) Using algebra, estimate the time and distance from Edinburgh at which the two trains pass one another.

Solutions are given on page 54.

Summary of Section 1

This section has reviewed or introduced:

- the slope of a straight line, which is 'rise $\div$ run' for any pair of points $A(x_1, y_1)$ and $B(x_2, y_2)$ on the line, where the run from A to B is $x_2 - x_1$ and the rise is $y_2 - y_1$;
- the equation $y = mx + c$, which represents a straight line in the (x, y)-plane that has slope m and y-intercept c;
- the equation $y - y_1 = m(x - x_1)$, which represents a straight line in the (x, y)-plane that has slope m and passes through the point (x_1, y_1);
- the fact that parallel lines have the same slope;
- the condition that if two lines are perpendicular, then *either* the product of their slopes is -1 *or* one has slope 0 and the other has infinite slope;
- the method for finding the point of intersection of two lines by solving the equations of the lines simultaneously.

Exercises for Section 1

Exercise 1.1

(a) Write down the rise and run from $(3,2)$ to $(-1,10)$.

(b) Calculate the slope of the line which passes through $(3,2)$ and $(-1,10)$.

(c) Find the equation of the line described in part (b).

(d) Find the x-intercept and y-intercept of the line described in part (b).

Exercise 1.2

Find the equation of the line that passes through the points $(2,3)$ and $(-1,-2)$.

Exercise 1.3

Find the equation of the line perpendicular to that in Exercise 1.2 which passes through the point $(2,3)$.

Exercise 1.4

Find the point of intersection of the two lines $y = 5x - 7$ and $y = -x + 11$.

2 Circles

To study Subsection 2.1 you will need a DVD player and DVD00104.

The video band indicates various ways of 'seeing circles' and illustrates some of their properties. In the remainder of Subsection 2.1, you will see how Pythagoras' Theorem leads to algebraic equations for circles. Subsection 2.2 demonstrates a method for finding the particular circle that passes through three specified points. Subsection 2.3 shows you how to tell whether a given algebraic equation describes a circle, and if so, which circle it describes. In Subsection 2.4 you will see how to locate any points at which a given line cuts a given circle.

2.1 Circles and their equations

Just as you have an intuitive idea of what the 'straightness' of a straight line involves, you probably have a good understanding of what the 'circularity' of a circle entails. The circle is, in a sense, the 'most perfect' of geometrical figures in a plane. Mathematically speaking, this 'perfection' can be tied down as follows.

Associated with any circle there is a special point called its **centre**. If the circle is either *rotated* through *any* angle about its centre, or *reflected* across any line through its centre, then the resulting figure occupies precisely the same position in the plane as the original circle. Only a circle possesses these features.

You will also be familiar with the idea that all points on a circle are at the same distance from its centre, and that this distance is called the **radius** of the circle. The video band refers to this and to other properties of circles.

Activity 2.1 Properties of circles

Now watch video band A(iii) on DVD00104, 'Visualising circles'.

If it is inconvenient to watch the video now, then continue with the text and view the video later.

The video band starts with an introduction that shows various occurrences of nearly circular shapes in the natural and manufactured worlds, and contrasts these with the 'ideal circle' which humans see in their minds. This is followed by four short episodes that address different properties of circles.

Comment

The four episodes in the video band are related to the following properties.

[1] *Points equidistant from a fixed point*

This leads to the best-known way of constructing a circle.

[2] *Three points fix a circle*

Arising from this fact, the centre of the circle that passes through three given points can be found by locating the intersection of the perpendicular bisectors of the line segments that join pairs of points. The radius of the circle is the distance from the centre to any of the three given points.

There is more about this construction in Subsection 2.2.

In the special case in which the three given points lie on a line, this construction breaks down, since the perpendicular bisectors are parallel to one another. In this case we can think of the 'centre' as being infinitely far away. In other words, a straight line can be regarded as a 'circle of infinite radius'.

[3] *Angles subtended by a fixed chord*

The angle made at a point on the circumference of a circle, by drawing lines to the point from both ends of a fixed chord (which is called the angle **subtended** by the chord at the point), is the same wherever on the circumference the point is chosen, provided that it is taken on the same side of the chord.

If the chord is not a diameter, then it subtends an *acute* angle (an angle between 0° and 90°) on the longer arc, and an *obtuse* angle (an angle between 90° and 180°) on the shorter arc (see Figure 2.1). These two angles add up to 180°. If the chord is a diameter, then both angles are exactly 90°.

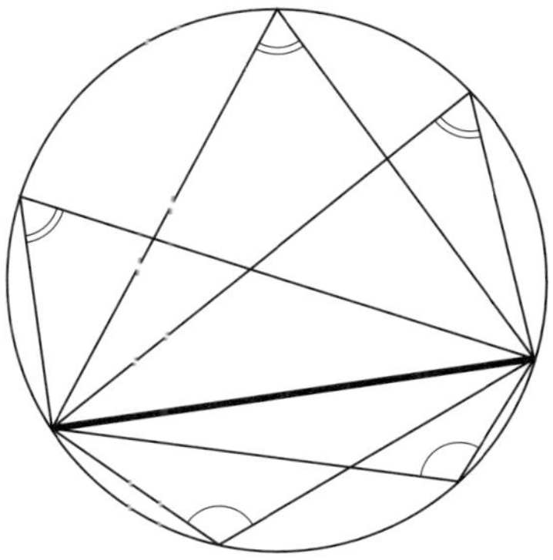

Figure 2.1
Subtended angles

[4] *Horizontal and vertical components*

The uniform movement of a point around a circle in a vertical plane can be seen as having two components: a vertical (or y-) component, showing the variable height of the point, and a horizontal (or x-) component, showing the side-to-side motion. The graph of each component with time has a similar 'wavy' shape. You will see later that for a circle with unit radius, these components are by definition the *sine* and *cosine* of the angle through which the point has travelled around the centre of the circle.

A fundamental result needed for the algebraic description of circles is *Pythagoras' Theorem*. Suppose that ABC is a right-angled triangle, with the right angle at C, as shown in Figure 2.2. The longest side of such a triangle, which is the side opposite the right angle, is called the *hypotenuse*. We denote by AB the length of the hypotenuse. Similarly, BC and AC represent the lengths of the other two sides of the triangle.

Pythagoras' Theorem states that in a right-angled triangle, the square of the hypotenuse is equal to the sum of the squares of the other two sides; that is,

$$AB^2 = AC^2 + BC^2.$$

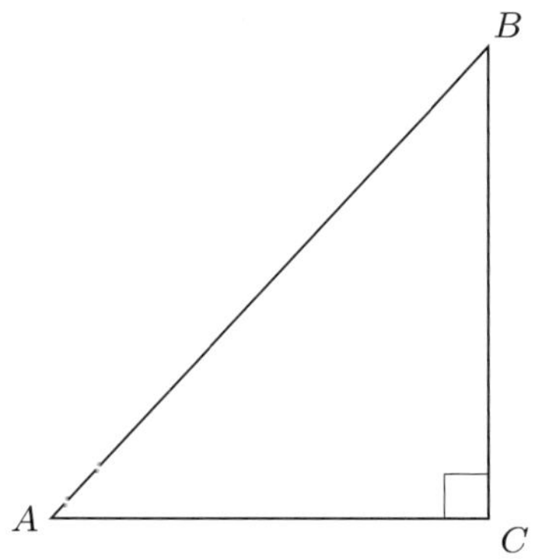

Figure 2.2
Right-angled triangle ABC

We are interested here in what the theorem tells us about the *distance* between two points. In Figure 2.2, the length AB is the distance from A to B, and according to Pythagoras' Theorem, this distance can be expressed in terms of the lengths AC and BC. Suppose that A has coordinates (x_1, y_1) and that B has coordinates (x_2, y_2). These points are shown in Figure 2.3, overleaf, together with the rise and run from A to B.

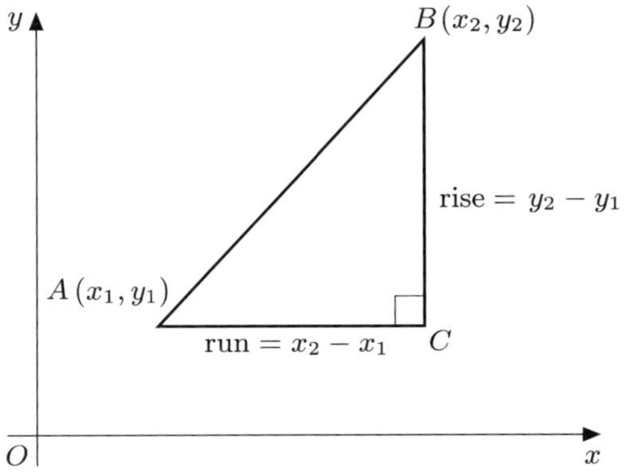

Figure 2.3 Rise and run from A to B

Here the line segment AB can be considered as the hypotenuse of a right-angled triangle whose other two sides have lengths equal to the magnitudes of the rise and the run, respectively. Applying Pythagoras' Theorem to this right-angled triangle gives

$$AB^2 = \text{run}^2 + \text{rise}^2.$$

Since the rise and run from A to B are given by run $= x_2 - x_1$ and rise $= y_2 - y_1$, we can deduce the following result.

Distance between two points

The distance AB between two points $A(x_1, y_1)$ and $B(x_2, y_2)$ is given by

$$AB^2 = (x_2 - x_1)^2 + (y_2 - y_1)^2.$$

Activity 2.2 Finding distances between pairs of points

Find the distance between each of the following pairs of points.

(a) $(3, 2)$ and $(7, 5)$ (b) $(-1, 4)$ and $(3, -2)$

Solutions are given on page 55.

The formula above for the distance between two points is the key to writing down an equation for a circle, since a defining property of a circle is that all points are at the same distance (the radius) from the centre.

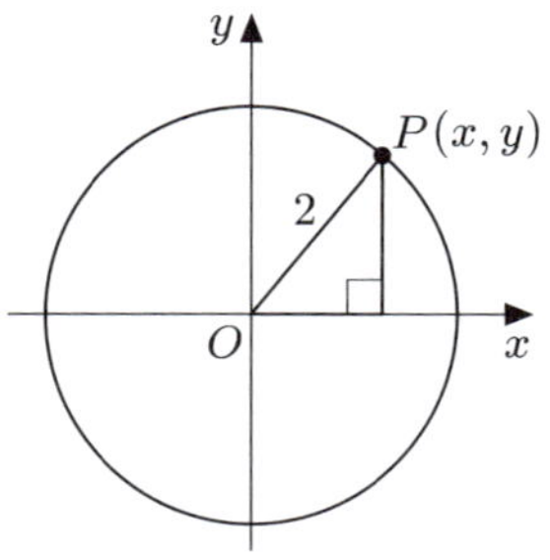

Figure 2.4 Circle with centre O and radius 2

Suppose, for example, that we seek an equation for the circle shown in Figure 2.4, which has centre at the origin O and radius 2. Suppose that $P(x, y)$ is any point on the circumference of this circle. Then the distance from O to P is $OP = 2$. According to the boxed formula above, we have

$$OP^2 = (x - 0)^2 + (y - 0)^2 = x^2 + y^2.$$

We deduce that $x^2 + y^2 = 4$. Hence the equation $x^2 + y^2 = 4$ describes precisely the circle with centre at the origin and radius 2, since a point lies on the circle only if its coordinates (x, y) satisfy this equation.

This argument generalises to any circle. The square of the distance from a fixed point (a, b) to any point (x, y) in the plane is given by $(x-a)^2 + (y-b)^2$. If (x, y) lies on the circle whose centre is (a, b) and whose radius is r, then the coordinates (x, y) must satisfy the equation

$$(x-a)^2 + (y-b)^2 = r^2.$$

The equation of a circle

The circle with centre (a, b) and radius r has equation

$$(x-a)^2 + (y-b)^2 = r^2.$$

For any particular circle, a, b and r are constants.

Activity 2.3 Writing down equations of circles

Write down the equation of the circle in the (x, y)-plane which satisfies each of the following specifications.

(a) Centre at $(0, 0)$, radius 3.

(b) Centre at $(5, 7)$, radius $\sqrt{2}$.

(c) Centre at $(-3, -1)$, radius 1.

Solutions are given on page 55.

Activity 2.4 Writing down the centre and radius

Write down the centre and radius of the circle specified by each of the following equations.

(a) $(x-1)^2 + (y-2)^2 = 25$

(b) $(x+1)^2 + (y+2)^2 = 49$

(c) $(x-\pi)^2 + (y+\pi)^2 = \pi^2$

(d) $x^2 + (y-\sqrt{3})^2 = 7$

Solutions are given on page 55.

2.2 Finding the circle through three points

As was pointed out during the Video Band, if three points are given which do not all lie on a single straight line, then there is a circle (and only one) that passes through all three points. You will now see how the centre and radius (and hence the equation) of this circle may be found, given the three points in coordinate form.

The basis of the method was referred to in the Comment for Activity 2.1, and is illustrated in Figure 2.5 overleaf.

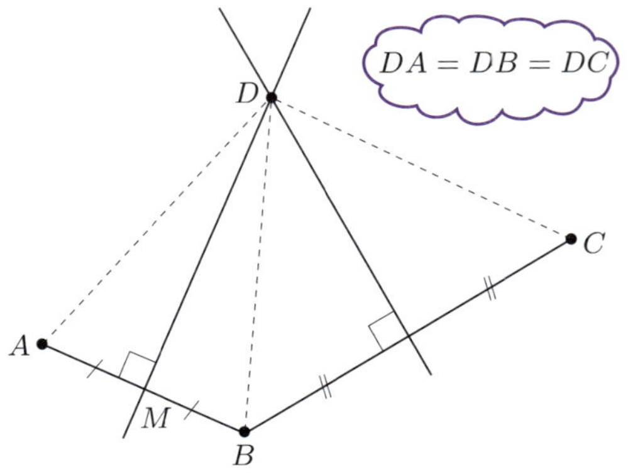

Figure 2.5 A, B and C define a circle

If fixed points A, B and C define a circle, then its centre D must be equidistant from them all.

The *line segment* AB comprises that part of the line through A and B which lies between A and B, including A and B themselves.

Now the points which are equidistant from A and B make up a line which cuts the line segment AB halfway along its length (at M, say) and is at right angles to AB. This line, shown as MD in Figure 2.5, is called the *perpendicular bisector* of AB.

Hence the centre D must lie on the perpendicular bisector of each of the line segments AB, BC and AC. Taking any two of these perpendicular bisectors (as drawn in Figure 2.5), the centre D is at their point of intersection. Once D has been located, the radius is the distance from D to any of the original three points.

This prescription involves finding the perpendicular bisector of a line segment between two given points, which passes through the midpoint of the line segment. We therefore need to start by obtaining the position of the midpoint, whose coordinates are given by the rule below.

Midpoint rule

The midpoint of the line segment between two points $A(x_1, y_1)$ and $B(x_2, y_2)$ has coordinates

$$\left(\tfrac{1}{2}(x_1 + x_2), \tfrac{1}{2}(y_1 + y_2)\right);$$

that is, its x-coordinate is the mean of the original x-coordinates, and its y-coordinate is the mean of the original y-coordinates.

The method described above is applied in a specific case in the following example.

Example 2.1 Finding the circle through three points

Find the centre and radius of the circle that passes through the three points $A(4, 8)$, $B(1, -1)$ and $C(-3, -3)$.

Solution

Let M, N be the midpoints of the line segments AB, BC, respectively, and let D be the centre of the circle (see Figure 2.6).

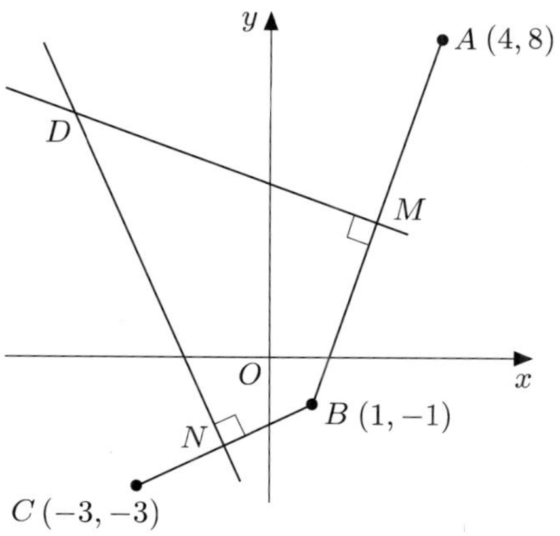

Figure 2.6 Finding the centre

The line segment AB has slope $(-1-8)\div(1-4)=3$ and midpoint M at

$$\left(\tfrac{1}{2}(4+1), \tfrac{1}{2}(8+(-1))\right) = \left(\tfrac{5}{2}, \tfrac{7}{2}\right).$$

Its perpendicular bisector MD therefore has slope $-\frac{1}{3}$ (using the perpendicularity condition from Subsection 1.1) and passes through $\left(\frac{5}{2}, \frac{7}{2}\right)$. Its equation is

$$y - \tfrac{7}{2} = -\tfrac{1}{3}\left(x - \tfrac{5}{2}\right); \quad \text{that is,} \quad y = -\tfrac{1}{3}x + \tfrac{13}{3}.$$

Similarly, the line segment BC has slope $(-3-(-1))\div(-3-1)=\frac{1}{2}$ and midpoint N at

$$\left(\tfrac{1}{2}(1+(-3)), \tfrac{1}{2}(-1+(-3))\right) = (-1, -2).$$

Its perpendicular bisector ND therefore has slope -2 and passes through $(-1,-2)$. Its equation is

$$y-(-2) = -2(x-(-1)); \quad \text{that is,} \quad y = -2x-4.$$

The two perpendicular bisectors, $y = -\frac{1}{3}x + \frac{13}{3}$ (MD) and $y=-2x-4$ (ND), intersect at D, where

$$-\tfrac{1}{3}x + \tfrac{13}{3} = -2x-4; \quad \text{that is,} \quad x=-5.$$

By substituting this value of x into the equation for ND, we find that the corresponding value of y is $y = -2\times(-5)-4=6$, so the centre D of the circle is at $(-5,6)$.

The radius r is the distance between D and A (or B, or C), so it is given by

$$r^2 = (4-(-5))^2 + (8-6)^2 = 85;$$

thus the radius is $r = \sqrt{85} \simeq 9.22$.

The resulting equation of the circle is $(x+5)^2+(y-6)^2=85$. As a check, this equation should be satisfied by the coordinates of each of A, B and C. For example, for B we have

$$(1+5)^2 + (-1-6)^2 = 36+49=85.$$

Another (rough) check is to sketch the positions of the four points A, B, C and D, as in Figure 2.6, and to verify that the coordinates found for D and the calculated radius look approximately correct.

Activity 2.5 Finding the circle through three points

By following the steps below, find the centre, radius and equation of the circle that passes through the three points $O(0,0)$, $A(-4,2)$ and $B(8,6)$.

(a) Show that the perpendicular bisector of OA has equation $y = 2x + 5$.

(b) Show that the perpendicular bisector of OB has equation $y = -\frac{4}{3}x + \frac{25}{3}$.

(c) By solving simultaneously the equations found in parts (a) and (b), find the centre of the circle.

(d) Use your answer to part (c) to find the radius of the circle.

(e) Write down the equation of the circle.

Solutions are given on page 55.

2.3 Completing the square

In Activity 2.3 you were asked to write down the equations of circles with given centre and radius. Although a 'standard form' for such equations has been given, they may also be expressed in different but equivalent ways. For example, the equation $x^2 + y^2 = 9$, for a circle with centre $(0,0)$ and radius 3, is equivalent to $2x^2 + 2y^2 = 18$, in which each term of the first equation has been multiplied by 2. Whenever the equation of a circle (or indeed of a line) is multiplied through by a non-zero multiple in this way, the resulting equation is an equivalent representation of the same circle (or line).

Similarly, we could rearrange the equation

$$(x-5)^2 + (y-7)^2 = 2 \quad \text{(for a circle with centre } (5,7) \text{ and radius } \sqrt{2})$$

by multiplying out the two brackets, to obtain

$$x^2 - 10x + 25 + y^2 - 14y + 49 = 2;$$

that is,

$$x^2 - 10x + y^2 - 14y + 72 = 0.$$

This equation describes the same circle, but it is no longer possible to 'read off' directly the coordinates of the centre and the value of the radius. However, an equation may be initially obtained in such a form, which raises the question of how you would then find the centre and radius from the equation. This question is now addressed.

The method required depends upon a technique known as **completing the square**. This is based on the algebraic identity

This identity appeared in Chapter A0, Section 4, in the form

$$(a+b)^2 = a^2 + 2ab + b^2.$$

$$x^2 + 2px + p^2 = (x+p)^2.$$

On subtracting the p^2 from both sides of the equation, we have

$$x^2 + 2px = (x+p)^2 - p^2.$$

The right-hand side is called the **completed-square form** of the left-hand side, since the variable x appears on the right only within a squared term. A term of this squared form is exactly what we seek in order to identify the x-coordinate of a circle's centre.

You will see another use of 'completing the square' in Subsection 4.1.

Example 2.2 Finding the centre and radius

Verify that the equation

$$x^2 + 4x + y^2 - 5y - 3 = 0$$

describes a circle, and find its centre and radius.

Solution

If we can find numbers a, b and r for which the equation given is equivalent to $(x-a)^2 + (y-b)^2 = r^2$, then we shall know that the equation does indeed describe a circle, with radius r and centre at (a, b).

First, consider the expression $x^2 + 4x$. Comparing this expression with the identity

$$x^2 + 2px = (x+p)^2 - p^2,$$

we can match $x^2 + 4x$ with the left-hand side by putting $2p = 4$: that is, $p = 2$. Putting this value also into the right-hand side, we obtain the completed-square form

$$x^2 + 4x = (x+2)^2 - 2^2 = (x+2)^2 - 4.$$

Now proceed similarly for the expression $y^2 - 5y$. With y in place of x, the general form is

$$y^2 + 2py = (y+p)^2 - p^2.$$

We can match $y^2 - 5y$ with the left-hand side by putting $2p = -5$, that is, $p = -\frac{5}{2}$. Putting this value also into the right-hand side, we obtain the completed-square form

$$y^2 - 5y = (y - \tfrac{5}{2})^2 - (-\tfrac{5}{2})^2 = (y - \tfrac{5}{2})^2 - \tfrac{25}{4}.$$

It remains to substitute both of the completed-square forms into the equation given, namely

$$x^2 + 4x + y^2 - 5y - 3 = 0.$$

In terms of the completed-square forms, this becomes

$$(x+2)^2 - 4 + (y - \tfrac{5}{2})^2 - \tfrac{25}{4} - 3 = 0.$$

On collecting the number terms and rearranging, we have

$$(x+2)^2 + (y - \tfrac{5}{2})^2 = \tfrac{53}{4}.$$

Hence the equation is indeed that of a circle, which has centre $(-2, \frac{5}{2})$ and radius $\frac{1}{2}\sqrt{53} \simeq 3.64$.

Activity 2.6 Finding the centre and radius

(a) Find the completed-square form of the expression $x^2 - 4x$.

(b) Find the completed-square form of the expression $y^2 - 6y$.

(c) Using your answers to parts (a) and (b), verify that the equation

$$x^2 - 4x + y^2 - 6y - 12 = 0$$

describes a circle, and find its centre and radius.

Solutions are given on page 55.

Note that not all equations involving $x^2 + y^2$, x, y and number terms will necessarily describe circles. To be a circle, the equation must be expressible as $(x-a)^2 + (y-b)^2$ equal to a *positive* quantity, namely r^2, the square of the radius of the circle. An example which is not of this pattern is $x^2 + y^2 = -1$. Since x^2 is not negative for any value of x, and similarly for y^2, there is no point in the plane which satisfies the condition $x^2 + y^2 = -1$. Another non-circle equation is $x^2 + y^2 = 0$. This is satisfied by the single point $(x, y) = (0, 0)$, and a single point is not usually regarded as a circle.

Hence $3x^2 + 2y^2 = 1$ is not the equation of a circle.

To have a chance of describing a circle, the equation must have the same coefficient for x^2 and y^2. In the examples considered so far, this coefficient has been chosen to be 1; if this is not initially the case, then it can be achieved by dividing through by the coefficient concerned.

For this reason, the formula which we derived earlier for completing the square is sufficient for the purpose of identifying the centre and radius of a circle given in general form. It also suffices to derive the formula for solution of a general quadratic equation, as is now shown.

The remainder of this subsection will not be assessed.

A general quadratic equation in the variable x has the form

$$ax^2 + bx + c = 0,$$

where a, b and c are constants. We assume that $a \neq 0$, since otherwise there is no quadratic term. On dividing through by a, we obtain

$$x^2 + \left(\frac{b}{a}\right)x + \frac{c}{a} = 0. \qquad (2.1)$$

The terms $x^2 + (b/a)x$ can be matched with the left-hand side of our previous 'completing the square' equation,

$$x^2 + 2px = (x+p)^2 - p^2.$$

The matching is achieved with $p = b/(2a)$, so we have

$$x^2 + \left(\frac{b}{a}\right)x = \left(x + \frac{b}{2a}\right)^2 - \frac{b^2}{4a^2}.$$

Thus equation (2.1) is equivalent to

$$\left(x + \frac{b}{2a}\right)^2 - \frac{b^2}{4a^2} + \frac{c}{a} = 0;$$

that is,

$$\left(x + \frac{b}{2a}\right)^2 = \frac{b^2}{4a^2} - \frac{c}{a} = \frac{b^2 - 4ac}{4a^2}.$$

Finally, we take the square root and then subtract $b/(2a)$ from both sides. This leads to the familiar formula

$$x = -\frac{b}{2a} \pm \sqrt{\frac{b^2 - 4ac}{4a^2}} = \frac{-b \pm \sqrt{b^2 - 4ac}}{2a}.$$

2.4 Intersections of circles and lines

You saw in Subsection 1.1 that if two non-parallel lines are represented by equations, then the intersection point of the lines may be found by solving their equations simultaneously. The same is true for other pairs of curves for which the equations are known.

In particular, we can find where a given line intersects a given circle. As with parallel lines, there may turn out to be no intersection point in some cases. For a line and a circle there are three possibilities, as illustrated in Figure 2.7.

Figure 2.7 Three possible cases

The line may intersect the circle in two distinct points, as shown in (a). Alternatively, it may touch the circle at a single point as in (b), in which case the line is a **tangent** to the circle. Thirdly, the line may not intersect the circle at all, as shown in (c).

When the equations of a line and a circle are solved simultaneously, the solution process leads to a *quadratic* equation, and the three cases that arise in solving such an equation (two real roots, one root or no real root) correspond to the three possible outcomes shown in Figure 2.7.

Example 2.3 Finding where line and circle meet

Find any points at which the circle $(x+7)^2 + (y-2)^2 = 80$ intersects each of the following lines.

Note that the three lines given are all parallel, since each has slope 2.

(a) $y = 2x - 4$

(b) $y = 2x$

(c) $y = 2x - 6$

Solution

(a) Using the equation of the line, $y = 2x - 4$, to substitute for y in the equation of the circle, we have

$$(x+7)^2 + (2x-4-2)^2 = 80.$$

On multiplying out the brackets and simplifying, we obtain the successive (equivalent) equations

$$(x+7)^2 + (2x-6)^2 = 80,$$
$$x^2 + 14x + 49 + 4x^2 - 24x + 36 = 80,$$
$$5x^2 - 10x + 5 = 0,$$
$$x^2 - 2x + 1 = 0.$$

The last equation factorises as $(x-1)^2 = 0$, which has the single solution $x = 1$. On feeding this value back into the equation of the line, we find $y = 2 \times 1 - 4 = -2$.

Hence the line is tangent to the circle at the point $(1, -2)$.

(b) The approach is the same as that in part (a). Substituting $y = 2x$ into the circle equation, we have

$$(x+7)^2 + (2x-2)^2 = 80,$$

which, after multiplying out the brackets and simplifying, reduces to

$$5x^2 + 6x - 27 = 0.$$

This equation factorises as $(x+3)(5x-9) = 0$, from which the solutions are $x = -3$ and $x = \frac{9}{5}$. Using each of these values in turn in the equation of the line, we obtain, respectively, $y = 2 \times (-3) = -6$ and $y = 2 \times \frac{9}{5} = \frac{18}{5}$.

The solutions can also be found using the formula for quadratic equations:

$$x = \frac{-6 \pm \sqrt{6^2 - 4\times 5\times(-27)}}{2\times 5} = \frac{-6\pm\sqrt{576}}{10} = \frac{-6\pm 24}{10}.$$

So $x = -3$ and $x = \frac{9}{5}$.

The line cuts the circle at the two points $(-3, -6)$ and $(\frac{9}{5}, \frac{18}{5})$.

(c) Proceeding as in parts (a) and (b), but this time with the line $y = 2x - 6$, we obtain

$$(x+7)^2 + (2x-8)^2 = 80.$$

This reduces to $5x^2 - 18x + 33 = 0$, which is of the form $ax^2 + bx + c = 0$ with $b^2 - 4ac = 18^2 - 4 \times 5 \times 33 = -336$. Since this is negative, the quadratic equation formula shows that there are no real roots.

Therefore there are no points which lie on both the line and the circle.

The positions of the circle and three lines are shown in Figure 2.8.

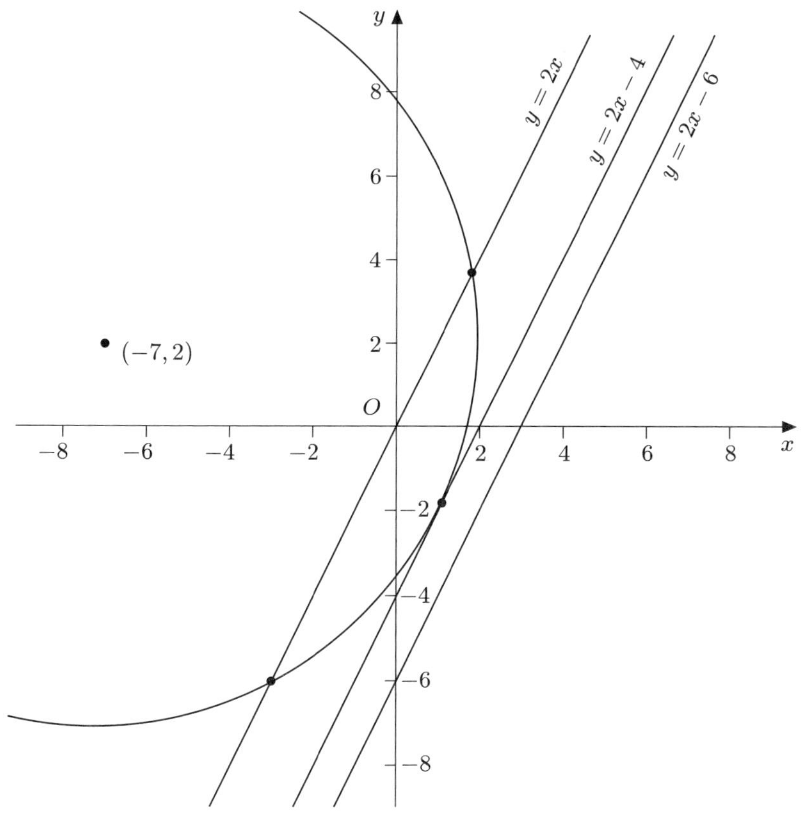

Figure 2.8 Intersection points

Activity 2.7 Finding where line and circle meet

Find any points at which the circle $(x-3)^2+(y+4)^2=53$ intersects the line $y=x+2$.

A solution is given on page 56.

If the line given is parallel to the x-axis, then the calculation becomes simpler. For example, the line $y=3$ meets the circle $(x-2)^2+(y+1)^2=25$ where

$$(x-2)^2+(3+1)^2=25; \quad \text{that is,} \quad (x-2)^2=25-16=9.$$

Hence we have $x-2=\pm 3$, so $x=5$ or $x=-1$. The points of intersection are $(5,3)$ and $(-1,3)$, since the line involved is $y=3$.

Similar simplification occurs if the given line is parallel to the y-axis, but here the quadratic equation to solve will be in terms of y rather than x.

You might wonder whether the solving simultaneous equations approach can also be applied to the problem of determining where (if at all) two circles intersect. It can: the method is illustrated briefly below. Consider the case of the two circles

The remainder of this subsection will not be assessed.

$$(x-3)^2+(y+4)^2=53 \quad \text{and} \quad (x+2)^2+(y-1)^2=13.$$

After multiplying out the brackets and simplifying, these equations become, respectively,

$$x^2-6x+y^2+8y-28=0,$$
$$x^2+4x+y^2-2y-8=0.$$

On subtracting the second equation from the first, we have

$$-10x+10y-20=0; \quad \text{that is,} \quad y=x+2,$$

which is the equation of a straight line. This line has the property that if A is a point lying on the line and one of the circles, then A also lies on the other circle. The intersection points of the two circles are therefore found by locating where the line meets either of the circles.

You showed in Activity 2.7 that this line meets the first of the circles given at the two points $(-4,-2)$ and $(1,3)$. Hence these are the two intersection points of the circles.

In general, as with a line and a circle, two circles may meet at two points, one point or no points. These three cases are illustrated in Figure 2.9. In each case, the line which is generated from the circles in the manner described above is drawn in. It is always perpendicular to the line joining the circle centres. Where the circles meet at a single point (case (b)), the line is a common tangent to the circles.

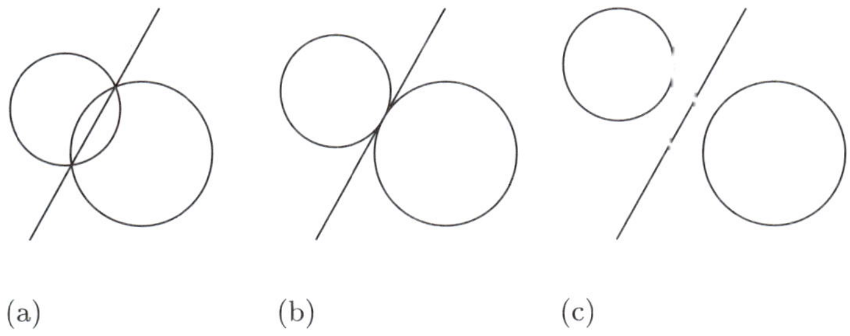

Figure 2.9 Three possible cases

Summary of Section 2

This section has introduced:

- ◇ the formula $AB^2 = (x_2 - x_1)^2 + (y_2 - y_1)^2$ giving the distance AB between two points $A(x_1, y_1)$ and $B(x_2, y_2)$;
- ◇ the equation $(x - a)^2 + (y - b)^2 = r^2$ to describe a circle with centre (a, b) and radius r;
- ◇ the coordinates $\left(\frac{1}{2}(x_1 + x_2), \frac{1}{2}(y_1 + y_2)\right)$ for the midpoint of the line segment between two points (x_1, y_1) and (x_2, y_2);
- ◇ the method for finding a circle through three given points;
- ◇ the completed-square form for $x^2 + 2px$, namely

  $$x^2 + 2px = (x + p)^2 - p^2,$$

  and its use, where necessary, in finding the centre and radius of a circle whose equation is given;
- ◇ the method for finding the points of intersection of a line and a circle, by solving their equations simultaneously.

Exercises for Section 2

Exercise 2.1

(a) Write down an equation which describes the circle with centre $(2, 3)$ and radius 4.

(b) Write down the centre and radius of the circle with equation

$$(x + 5)^2 + (y - 4)^2 = 17.$$

Exercise 2.2

Find the centre and radius of the circle which passes through the three points $A(-2, 2)$, $B(-1, 0)$ and $C(1, 6)$. Write down the equation of the circle.

Exercise 2.3

(a) Find the completed-square form of the expression $x^2 + 14x$.

(b) Find the completed-square form of the expression $y^2 - 24y$.

(c) Using your answers to parts (a) and (b), verify that the equation

$$x^2 + 14x + y^2 - 24y - 96 = 0$$

describes a circle, and find its centre and radius.

Exercise 2.4

Find any points at which the circle $(x - 3)^2 + (y + 7)^2 = 65$ intersects the line $y = \frac{3}{2}x + \frac{3}{2}$.

3 Trigonometry

Trigonometry is concerned with various ratios of lengths that are associated with angles. In Subsection 3.1 you will see definitions of two of these ratios, the *sine* and *cosine*, together with some of their basic properties. Subsection 3.2 then explains how the sine and cosine may be put to use within triangles, for the purpose of deducing lengths from angle sizes or vice versa.

It is assumed that you have come across most of the topics in this section previously. They will be covered quite rapidly.

3.1 Sine and cosine

Consider the circle shown in Figure 3.1. This circle has radius 1 and centre at the origin, O. It is often called the **unit circle**.

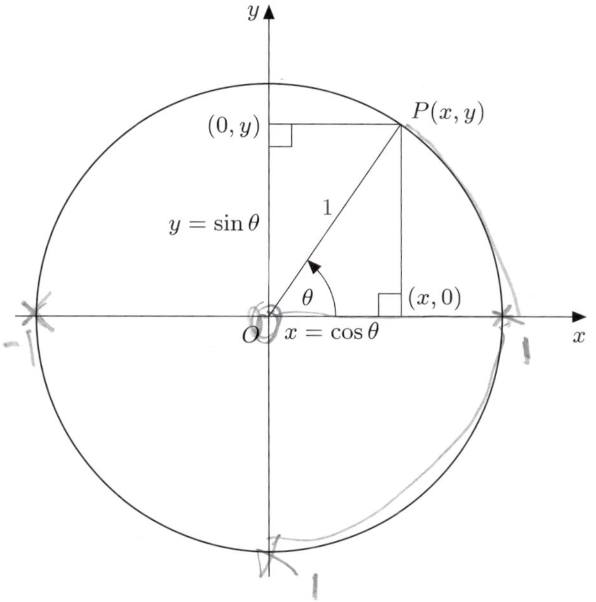

Figure 3.1 The unit circle

Consider the point P on the circumference of the unit circle, placed so that the angle between the positive x-axis and the line segment OP, measured anticlockwise, is θ, where θ is positive.

If θ is negative, then P is placed by rotating clockwise from the positive x-axis through the angle $-\theta$.

Suppose now that P has coordinates (x, y). This is the same as saying that the vertical line through P meets the x-axis at $(x, 0)$, and the horizontal line through P meets the y-axis at $(0, y)$, as marked. Then the **cosine** and **sine** of the angle θ are defined by

$$\cos\theta = x, \quad \sin\theta = y.$$

These definitions apply to all values of θ – negative, zero and positive.

The angle θ may be measured either in *degrees* (360° per complete revolution) or in *radians* (2π radians per complete revolution). We shall use radians for the moment, but switch to degrees in the context of triangles in Subsection 3.2.

As an example of applying the definitions of cosine and sine, suppose that $\theta = \frac{1}{2}\pi$. Then P has coordinates $(0, 1)$, so $\cos(\frac{1}{2}\pi) = 0$ and $\sin(\frac{1}{2}\pi) = 1$.

Activity 3.1 Values of cos and sin

By placing P at appropriate points on the unit circle, find the values of the following.

(a) $\cos 0$ and $\sin 0$ (b) $\cos(-\frac{1}{2}\pi)$ and $\sin(-\frac{1}{2}\pi)$ (c) $\cos \pi$ and $\sin \pi$

Solutions are given on page 56.

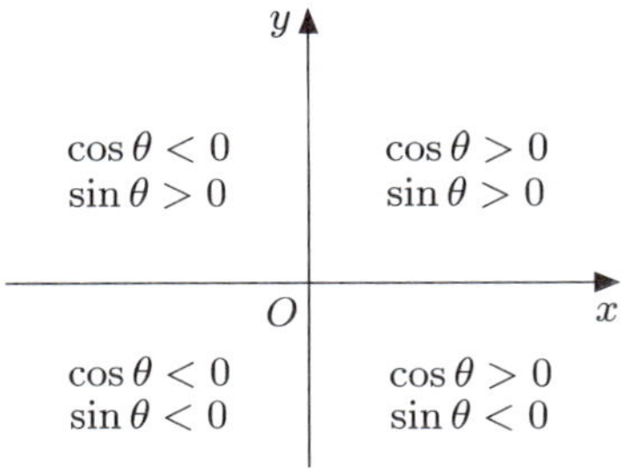

Figure 3.2
Signs in quadrants

The values of sine and cosine may be positive, negative or zero, depending where on the circle P lies. The signs of these trigonometric quantities within the four *quadrants* of the plane (the four parts separated by the axes) are as shown in Figure 3.2. These follow directly from the signs of the x- and y-coordinates in these quadrants.

Certain formulas which relate the sines and cosines of angles may be derived by looking at the geometry of points on the unit circle. Note first that the position of P is unaffected if the angle θ is increased or decreased by a complete revolution. In symbols, this may be expressed as

These identities are valid for all values of θ.

$$\cos(\theta + 2\pi) = \cos\theta \quad \text{and} \quad \sin(\theta + 2\pi) = \sin\theta,$$

which says that the values of both cosine and sine repeat themselves every 2π radians.

Consider now the effect of reflecting points on the circle across the x-axis, as shown in Figure 3.3(a). If the point $P(x, y)$ corresponds to the angle θ, and the point Q is the reflection of P in the x-axis, then Q has coordinates $(x, -y)$ and corresponds to the angle $-\theta$. Hence we have

$$\cos(-\theta) = \cos\theta \quad \text{and} \quad \sin(-\theta) = -\sin\theta.$$

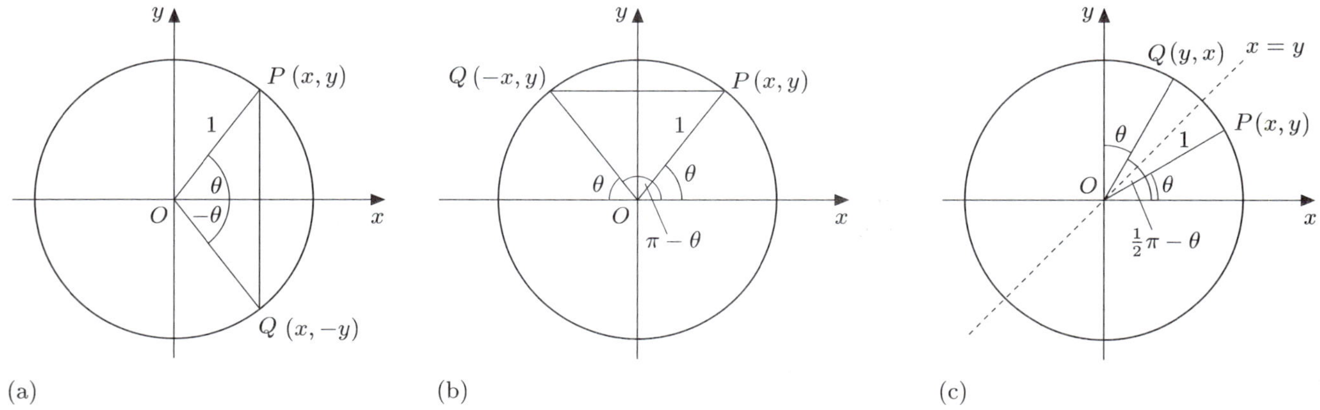

Figure 3.3 Reflections

Similarly, the case of reflection in the y-axis (see Figure 3.3(b), where the point Q corresponds to the angle $\pi - \theta$) gives

$$\cos(\pi - \theta) = -\cos\theta \quad \text{and} \quad \sin(\pi - \theta) = \sin\theta.$$

Further useful identities are obtained by considering reflection in the line $x = y$ (see Figure 3.3(c)). These are

Here the point Q corresponds to the angle $\frac{1}{2}\pi - \theta$.

$$\cos(\tfrac{1}{2}\pi - \theta) = \sin\theta \quad \text{and} \quad \sin(\tfrac{1}{2}\pi - \theta) = \cos\theta.$$

Another key property of sine and cosine follows from the fact that P lies on the unit circle, so its coordinates satisfy the equation $x^2 + y^2 = 1$. Hence, for any value of θ, we have

Note that we write $\cos^2\theta$ for $(\cos\theta)^2$ and $\sin^2\theta$ for $(\sin\theta)^2$.

$$\cos^2\theta + \sin^2\theta = 1.$$

Activity 3.2 More values of cos and sin

(a) By applying the formula

$$\cos(\tfrac{1}{2}\pi - \theta) = \sin\theta,$$

show that $\cos\left(\frac{1}{4}\pi\right) = \sin\left(\frac{1}{4}\pi\right)$. Then use the formula

$$\cos^2\theta + \sin^2\theta = 1$$

to find the common value of $\cos(\frac{1}{4}\pi)$ and $\sin(\frac{1}{4}\pi)$.

(b) By considering the geometry of the diagram in Figure 3.4, in which $\triangle OPQ$ is an equilateral triangle bisected by the x-axis, find the values of $\cos(\frac{1}{6}\pi)$ and $\sin(\frac{1}{6}\pi)$.

The symbol $\triangle$ is read as 'triangle'.

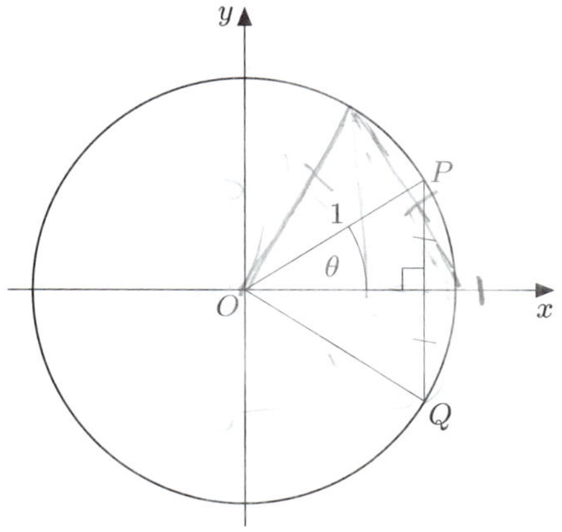

Figure 3.4 Triangle OPQ

(c) What are the values of $\cos(\frac{1}{3}\pi)$ and $\sin(\frac{1}{3}\pi)$?

Solutions are given on page 56.

The values of the sine and cosine of any angle (expressed in either degrees or radians) may be obtained rapidly from a calculator, but values for the particular angles in Activities 3.1 and 3.2 crop up often enough to make it worth committing them to memory if possible.

If this is too daunting a prospect, then these values can be looked up in the Handbook.

Imagine now that the point P in Figure 3.1 rotates at a steady rate around the circle. The corresponding values of $\cos\theta$ and $\sin\theta$ (the coordinates of P) oscillate up and down between -1 and 1. You saw in the Video Band in Subsection 2.1 (from which a still is reproduced in Figure 3.5) the 'wavy' graphs that result.

You will see more about these graphs in Chapter A3.

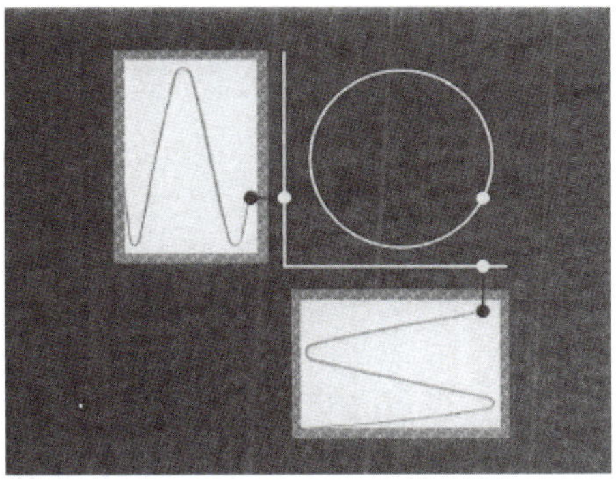

Figure 3.5 Wavy graphs

We now define a third trigonometric ratio, the **tangent** of an angle. It is defined by

$$\tan\theta = \frac{\sin\theta}{\cos\theta},$$

which makes sense only if $\cos\theta \neq 0$. In terms of Figure 3.1, this is equivalent to $\tan\theta = y/x$ $(x \neq 0)$, so $\tan\theta$ is undefined if the point P lies on the y-axis (that is, for $\theta = \pm\frac{1}{2}\pi, \pm\frac{3}{2}\pi, \pm\frac{5}{2}\pi, \ldots$). Note that if a line makes an angle θ measured anticlockwise from the positive x-axis, then $\tan\theta$ is the *slope* of the line, as defined in Subsection 1.1.

The value $\theta = \frac{1}{2}\pi$, for which the tangent is undefined, corresponds to lines of infinite slope.

Activity 3.3 Values of tan

Find the value of each of the following.

(a) $\tan 0$ (b) $\tan\pi$ (c) $\tan(\frac{1}{4}\pi)$ (d) $\tan(\frac{1}{6}\pi)$ (e) $\tan(\frac{1}{3}\pi)$

Solutions are given on page 56.

It follows from the corresponding formulas for cos and sin that

$$\tan(-\theta) = \frac{\sin(-\theta)}{\cos(-\theta)} = \frac{-\sin\theta}{\cos\theta} = -\tan\theta$$

and

$$\tan(\pi - \theta) = \frac{\sin(\pi-\theta)}{\cos(\pi-\theta)} = \frac{\sin\theta}{-\cos\theta} = -\tan\theta.$$

The tangent is positive where both cosine and sine are positive or where they are both negative. Figure 3.6 indicates which of sin, cos and tan are positive in each quadrant.

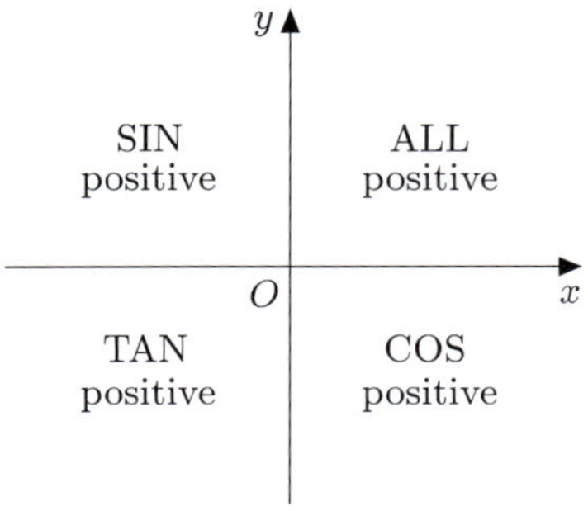

Figure 3.6
Signs in quadrants

Activity 3.4 Values of sin, cos and tan

Use the formulas for sin, cos and tan and the solutions to Activities 3.2 and 3.3 to find the value of each of the following.

(a) $\sin(\frac{5}{6}\pi)$ (b) $\cos(\frac{5}{6}\pi)$ (c) $\tan(\frac{2}{3}\pi)$ (d) $\tan(-\frac{1}{3}\pi)$

Solutions are given on page 56.

To conclude this subsection, three further trigonometric ratios, the secant, cosecant and cotangent of an angle, are defined by

$$\sec\theta = \frac{1}{\cos\theta}, \quad \operatorname{cosec}\theta = \frac{1}{\sin\theta}, \quad \cot\theta = \frac{1}{\tan\theta}.$$

These are sometimes used when we wish to avoid reciprocals.

For example,
$\sec\left(\frac{1}{6}\pi\right) = 2/\sqrt{3} = \frac{2}{3}\sqrt{3}$,
$\operatorname{cosec}\left(\frac{1}{4}\pi\right) = \sqrt{2}$,
$\cot\left(\frac{1}{3}\pi\right) = 1/\sqrt{3} = \frac{1}{3}\sqrt{3}$.

3.2 Calculations with triangles

Figure 3.7 shows an amended copy of the diagram (Figure 3.1) referred to when defining cosine and sine. The line segment OP is extended to some point A, and a perpendicular is dropped from A to the x-axis at B. Here it is assumed that θ is acute, that is, between 0 and $\pi/2$ radians (90°).

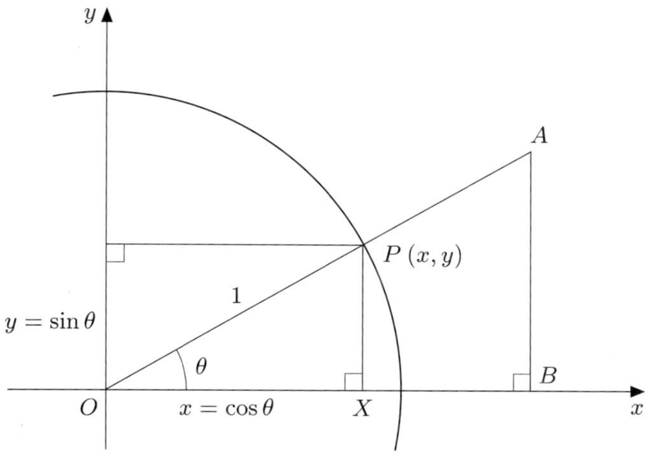

Figure 3.7 Defining A and B

Since $\triangle OAB$ and $\triangle OPX$ are similar, it follows that

$$\frac{OB}{OA} = \frac{OX}{OP} = \frac{x}{1} = x = \cos\theta,$$

and similarly that $AB/OA = \sin\theta$, whatever the size of the right-angled triangle OAB.

Now consider $\triangle OAB$ on its own (Figure 3.8(a)). The side OA is the hypotenuse of the triangle. The side OB is *adjacent* to the angle θ, and the side AB is *opposite* to the angle θ.

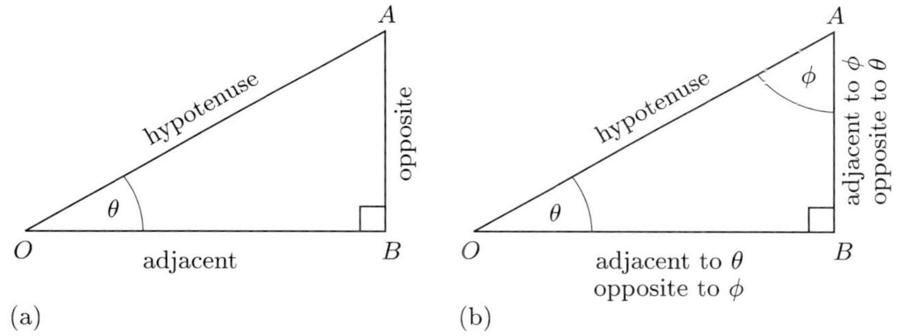

Figure 3.8 Adjacent, opposite, hypotenuse

This gives, for an angle θ within a right-angled triangle, the formulas

$$\cos\theta = \frac{\text{adjacent}}{\text{hypotenuse}}, \quad \sin\theta = \frac{\text{opposite}}{\text{hypotenuse}}, \quad \tan\theta = \frac{\text{opposite}}{\text{adjacent}}.$$

These formulas are often used to introduce the cosine and sine.

Note that both of the descriptions 'adjacent' and 'opposite' are relative to the angle currently under consideration. Indeed, if ϕ is the third angle in the triangle, as shown in Figure 3.8(b), then

$$\cos\phi = \frac{\text{adjacent (to } \phi)}{\text{hypotenuse}} = \frac{\text{opposite (to } \theta)}{\text{hypotenuse}} = \sin\theta,$$

and, similarly, $\sin\phi = \cos\theta$.

These are instances of general rules from Subsection 3.1, namely

$$\cos(\tfrac{1}{2}\pi - \theta) = \sin\theta,$$
$$\sin(\tfrac{1}{2}\pi - \theta) = \cos\theta,$$

since $\phi = \frac{1}{2}\pi - \theta$.

These relationships mean that, in any *right-angled* triangle, the specification of either

(a) one other angle and the length of any one side, or

(b) the lengths of any two sides

is sufficient to enable us to determine all angles and side lengths of the triangle. This process is often called *solving the triangle*.

Activity 3.5 Solving triangles

The inverse sine of a number gives an angle whose sine is that number (where this is possible), and similarly for the inverse cosine.

Find the unmarked angles and lengths of sides in each of the two triangles in Figure 3.9 below. In part (b) you will need to apply the 'inverse sine' or 'inverse cosine' facility on your calculator. (Make sure that your calculator is set to work in degrees.)

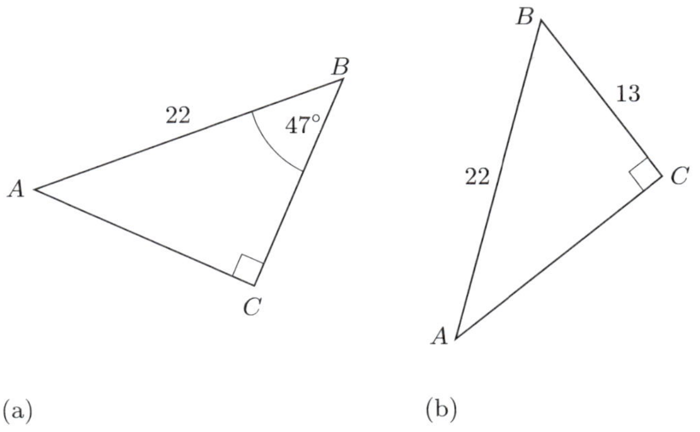

Figure 3.9 Two triangles

Solutions are given on page 57.

The remainder of this subsection will not be assessed.

To conclude this subsection, there follows a brief indication of how trigonometry can also be applied to solve triangles such as that shown in Figure 3.10(a), which do *not* contain a right angle. This illustrates a standard convention for labelling the angles and side lengths of a triangle, with length a opposite $\angle A$, length b opposite $\angle B$, and length c opposite $\angle C$.

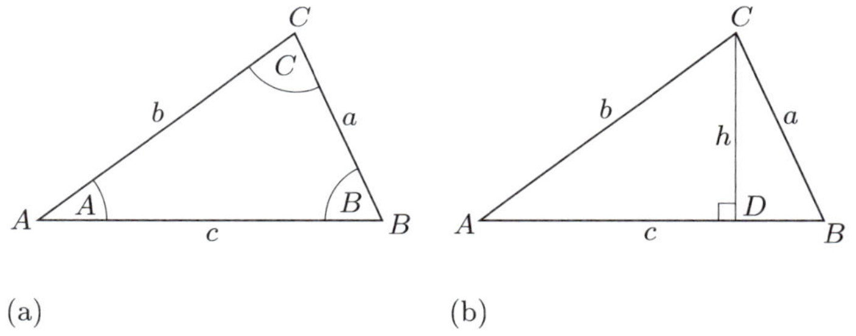

Figure 3.10 A labelling convention

The rules for solving such triangles depend essentially upon being able to view them as being made up of right-angled triangles. For example, by dropping the perpendicular from C to AB in $\triangle ABC$, we divide this triangle into two smaller ones with right angles, $\triangle ADC$ and $\triangle CDB$, as shown in Figure 3.10(b). Denoting the length of CD by h, we have $h = b \sin A$ (in $\triangle ADC$) and $h = a \sin B$ (in $\triangle CDB$). It follows that

In full, the sine rule is

$$\frac{\sin A}{a} = \frac{\sin B}{b} = \frac{\sin C}{c}.$$

$$\frac{\sin A}{a} = \frac{\sin B}{b},$$

which is known as the **sine rule**. Given the length of one side for any triangle whose angles are known, this rule permits us to deduce the lengths of the remaining sides.

Summary of Section 3

This section has reviewed or introduced:

- the definitions $\cos\theta = x$, $\sin\theta = y$, where (x, y) are the coordinates of a point P on the unit circle such that the angle from the positive x-axis to OP is θ;
- the following properties of cos and sin:

$$\cos(\theta + 2\pi) = \cos\theta, \quad \sin(\theta + 2\pi) = \sin\theta,$$
$$\cos(-\theta) = \cos\theta, \quad \sin(-\theta) = -\sin\theta,$$
$$\cos(\pi - \theta) = -\cos\theta, \quad \sin(\pi - \theta) = \sin\theta,$$
$$\cos(\tfrac{1}{2}\pi - \theta) = \sin\theta, \quad \sin(\tfrac{1}{2}\pi - \theta) = \cos\theta,$$
$$\cos^2\theta + \sin^2\theta = 1;$$

- the definition $\tan\theta = \sin\theta/(\cos\theta)$, where $\cos\theta \neq 0$, together with the properties

$$\tan(-\theta) = -\tan\theta, \quad \tan(\pi - \theta) = -\tan\theta;$$

- the definitions $\sec\theta = 1/(\cos\theta)$, $\operatorname{cosec}\theta = 1/(\sin\theta)$ and $\cot\theta = 1/(\tan\theta)$, where in each case the denominators are non-zero;
- within a right-angled triangle having acute angle θ, the formulas

$$\cos\theta = \frac{\text{adjacent}}{\text{hypotenuse}}, \quad \sin\theta = \frac{\text{opposite}}{\text{hypotenuse}}, \quad \tan\theta = \frac{\text{opposite}}{\text{adjacent}}.$$

Exercises for Section 3

Exercise 3.1

(a) Replace θ by $-\theta$ in the formulas

$$\cos(\pi - \theta) = -\cos\theta, \quad \sin(\pi - \theta) = \sin\theta.$$

Hence derive formulas for

$\cos(\theta + \pi)$ in terms of $\cos\theta$,
$\sin(\theta + \pi)$ in terms of $\sin\theta$.

(b) Use these formulas to find the value of each of the following.

(i) $\sin(\frac{7}{6}\pi)$ (ii) $\cos(\frac{7}{6}\pi)$ (iii) $\tan(\frac{7}{6}\pi)$

Exercise 3.2

Find the unmarked angles and lengths of sides in each of the two triangles in Figure 3.11 below.

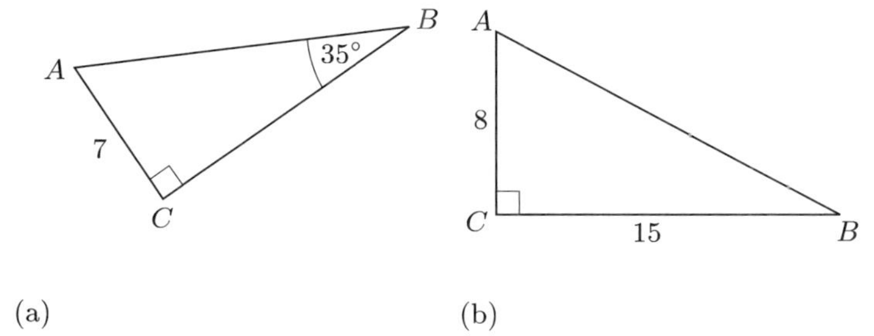

Figure 3.11 Two triangles

4 Parametric equations

In Sections 1 and 2, you saw how equations which relate the x- and y-coordinates of a point provide an algebraic description of a line or a circle. In this section you will see an alternative way of doing this. In place of the single equation for a line or circle employed previously, we use two equations, which express each of x and y in terms of a further variable, say t, called the *parameter* for the equations.

You can think of the two equations as telling you the position (x, y) of a small object at time t, as the object moves along a line or circle. The apparent extra complexity of introducing a third variable, t, is offset by additional information: you know not only the path along which the object moves, but also its position on the path at any particular time.

We look in Subsection 4.1 at parametric equations for lines and in Subsection 4.2 at parametric equations for circles.

4.1 Parametric equations of lines

Consider the equation $y = 2x + 3$, which describes a particular straight line. This says that the y-coordinate of any point on the line must equal twice the x-coordinate of that point, plus 3. Another way of specifying this is to say that all points on the line have coordinates of the form $(x, 2x + 3)$, where x is any real number. We could equally well use another letter here in place of x, for example, t. Then the line consists of all points of the form $(t, 2t + 3)$, which in turn says that the line is made up of points (x, y) such that

$$x = t, \quad y = 2t + 3.$$

Unless t is explicitly limited in some way, it is to be assumed in such equations that t takes all real values. Note that the use of 'parameter' here is different from that in Chapter A1.

The additional variable t which has been introduced is called a **parameter**, and the two equations are called **parametric equations**. The process of describing x and y in terms of t is called **parametrisation** of the original line.

The equations $x = t$, $y = 2t + 3$ represent just one way of parametrising the line $y = 2x + 3$. For example, if we returned to the coordinate form $(x, 2x + 3)$, and then replaced x by $4t + 1$, we would arrive at another valid parametrisation:

$$x = 4t + 1, \quad y = 2(4t + 1) + 3 = 8t + 5.$$

Why should we want to do this? On the face of it, such pairs of equations are a more complicated description of the line than the single equation, $y = 2x + 3$, from which we started. However, we have also potentially gained information that could be useful in a modelling context. If t represents time, and $x = 4t + 1$, $y = 8t + 5$ represent the coordinates of a moving object, then we can say that when $t = 0$ the object is at $(1, 5)$, when $t = \frac{1}{2}$ it is at $(3, 9)$, and so on. For each chosen time, there is a corresponding position on the line.

Figure 4.1 illustrates the above two parametrisations of the line $y = 2x + 3$.

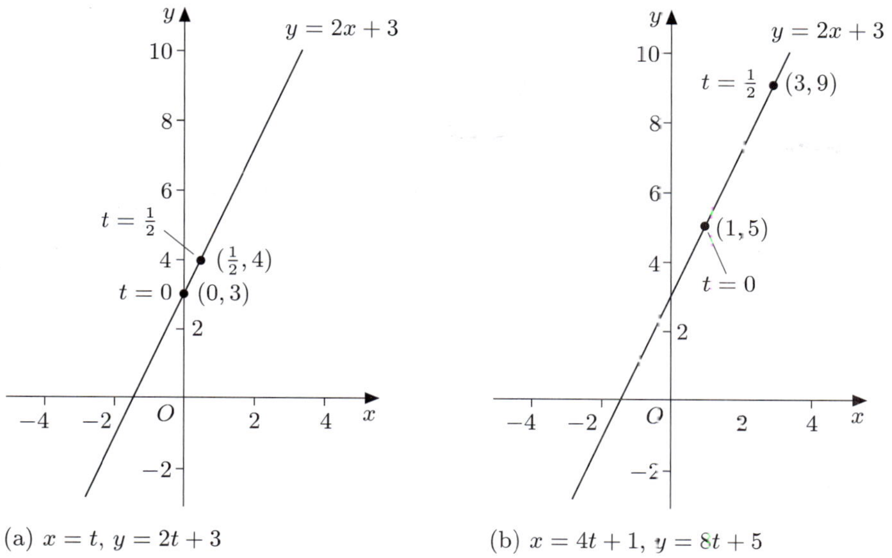

Figure 4.1 Two parametrisations of one line

In Subsection 1.1, you saw how to obtain the equation of a line specified by either of

(a) the slope of the line and one point on it;

(b) two points on the line.

In each case, an appropriate parametrisation of the line is as follows.

You may like to check that these two parametrisations work, by substituting them into the appropriate form of the equation of a line.

(a) If a line in the (x, y)-plane has slope m and passes through the point (x_1, y_1), then it can be parametrised as

$$x = t + x_1, \quad y = mt + y_1.$$

Here $(x, y) = (x_1, y_1)$ when $t = 0$. The parameter t is the run from (x_1, y_1) to (x, y).

(b) If a line in the (x, y)-plane passes through the two points (x_1, y_1) and (x_2, y_2), then it can be parametrised as

$$x = x_1 + t(x_2 - x_1), \quad y = y_1 + t(y_2 - y_1).$$

Here $(x, y) = (x_1, y_1)$ when $t = 0$, and $(x, y) = (x_2, y_2)$ when $t = 1$. The magnitude of the parameter t gives the distance from (x_1, y_1) to (x, y) as a proportion of the distance from (x_1, y_1) to (x_2, y_2).

This parametrisation is illustrated in Figure 4.2.

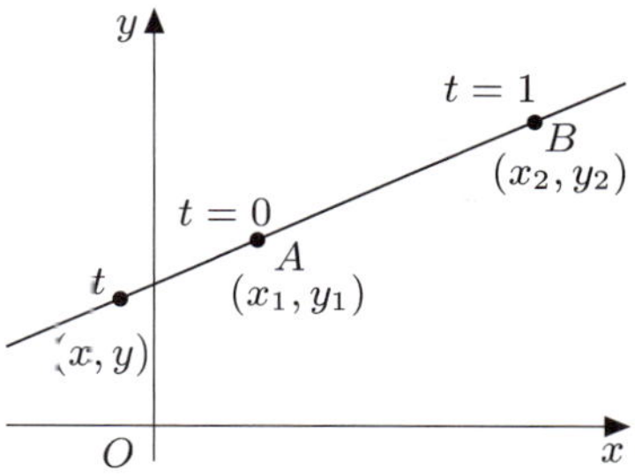

Figure 4.2 Case (b)

Note that the midpoint of the line segment from $A(x_1, y_1)$ to $B(x_2, y_2)$ corresponds to the parameter value $t = \frac{1}{2}$ (see Figure 4.3). Putting $t = \frac{1}{2}$ into the parametric equations above gives the midpoint formula stated in Subsection 2.2, namely,

$$(x, y) = \left(\tfrac{1}{2}(x_1 + x_2), \tfrac{1}{2}(y_1 + y_2)\right).$$

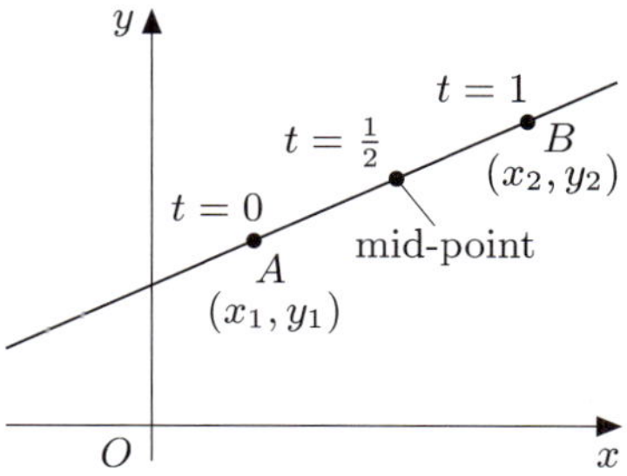

Figure 4.3 Midpoint

Activity 4.1 Parametric equations for specified lines

Write down parametric equations for:

(a) the line which has slope 3 and passes through the point $(1, -2)$;

(b) the line which passes through the two points $(1, 5)$ and $(4, -7)$.

Solutions are given on page 57.

In this context, it is sometimes useful to describe the equation $y = mx + c$ as the 'non-parametric form'.

From parametric equations for a line, the equation $y = mx + c$ can be found by eliminating the parameter t between the pair of equations.

Example 4.1 Eliminating the parameter

From the parametric equations $x = t + 1$, $y = 3t - 2$, deduce the equation of the corresponding line.

Solution

If $x = t + 1$, then $t = x - 1$. Hence we have

$$y = 3t - 2 = 3(x - 1) - 2 = 3x - 5;$$

that is, the equation of the line is $y = 3x - 5$.

Activity 4.2 Eliminating the parameter

From the parametric equations $x = 3t + 1$, $y = -12t + 5$, deduce the equation of the corresponding line.

A solution is given on page 57.

A type of problem that can be tackled using coordinates given in terms of a parameter is illustrated below.

Example 4.2 Closest approach

Two ships pursue straight-line courses at steady speeds. With reference to a given Cartesian coordinate system, the position of Ship 1 is $(3t - 10, t + 4)$ and the position of Ship 2 is $(2t - 3, -t + 13)$, both in terms of time t. Here distance is measured in kilometres and time in hours. What is the closest that the ships approach each other, and at what time does this closest approach occur?

Solution

Here we apply the formula from Subsection 2.1 for the distance between two points.

At time t, the distance d between the two ships is given by

$$d^2 = (3t - 10 - (2t - 3))^2 + (t + 4 - (-t + 13))^2.$$

The closest approach occurs when d^2 (and hence d) takes its minimum value, but this cannot be identified from the expression as it stands. We start, therefore, by rearranging it in stages:

$$\begin{aligned} d^2 &= (t - 7)^2 + (2t - 9)^2 \\ &= t^2 - 14t + 49 + 4t^2 - 36t + 81 \\ &= 5t^2 - 50t + 130 \\ &= 5(t^2 - 10t) + 130. \end{aligned}$$

We require the minimum value of d^2. In order to find it, we apply the 'completing the square' formula, from Subsection 2.3, to the expression in brackets. This gives

$$d^2 = 5((t - 5)^2 - 25) + 130 = 5(t - 5)^2 + 5.$$

The term $5(t-5)^2$ never takes a value less than 0, and it achieves the value 0 when $t=5$. At this time, the value of d^2 is 5. Hence the closest approach distance is $\sqrt{5} \simeq 2.24$ (km), and this occurs when $t=5$ (hours).

No square of a real number is negative.

Activity 4.3 Closest approach

Two aircraft fly along straight-line courses at the same height and at steady speeds. With reference to a given Cartesian coordinate system, the position of Aircraft 1 is $(500t+10, -312t-12)$ and the position of Aircraft 2 is $(496t+22, -310t-23)$, both in terms of time t. Here distance is measured in kilometres and time in hours. What is the closest that the aircraft approach each other, and at what time does this closest approach occur?

A solution is given on page 57.

If we want to specify only *part* of a line, then this can be achieved by restricting the parameter to only certain real values. For example, it was pointed out earlier that the line joining $A(x_1, y_1)$ and $B(x_2, y_2)$ can be parametrised as

$$x = x_1 + t(x_2 - x_1), \quad y = y_1 + t(y_2 - y_1),$$

Note that if t is replaced here by $1-t$, then the new parametrisation describes the same line but traversed in the opposite direction, with $t=0$ at (x_2, y_2) and $t=1$ at (x_1, y_1).

where $(x,y) = (x_1, y_1)$ at $t=0$ and $(x,y) = (x_2, y_2)$ at $t=1$. As they stand, these equations apply for all real numbers t, and represent a line which extends infinitely far in either direction. To describe just the line *segment* from A to B, we could add the condition that t should be no less than 0 and no greater than 1. In symbols, this can be written as $0 \le t \le 1$, which is read as '0 less than or equal to t, and t less than or equal to 1'. The equations then read

$$x = x_1 + t(x_2 - x_1), \quad y = y_1 + t(y_2 - y_1) \quad (0 \le t \le 1).$$

4.2 Parametric equations of circles

In the case of circles, we have a ready parametrisation suggested by the video animation which was illustrated in Figure 3.5. The equations

$$x = \cos\theta, \quad y = \sin\theta$$

provide a parametrisation of the unit circle, with the angle θ as the parameter (see Figure 3.1). The angle θ here can be replaced by t (time), but equally it could be replaced by $2t$, $3t$ or any non-zero multiple of t. These each describe a moving point which traces out the same circular path, but they differ in the rate at which the point rotates. To be more specific, all parametrisations of the form

$$x = \cos(kt), \quad y = \sin(kt),$$

where k is a non-zero constant, represent the unit circle. For $k=1$ (that is, $\theta = t$), points on the circle are reached at the times indicated in Figure 4.4(a). The motion is in the anticlockwise direction, since we have assumed that angles increase in this direction. For $k=2$ (that is, $\theta = 2t$), motion takes place at twice the rate, reaching $\theta = \frac{1}{4}\pi$ at $t = \frac{1}{8}\pi$, $\theta = \frac{1}{2}\pi$ at $t = \frac{1}{4}\pi$, and so on (see Figure 4.4(b)). For $k = \frac{1}{2}$ (that is, $\theta = \frac{1}{2}t$), the rate of motion is only a half that with $\theta = t$ (see Figure 4.4(c)). In each anticlockwise revolution, θ increases by 2π (radians), and hence the time t increases by $2\pi/k$.

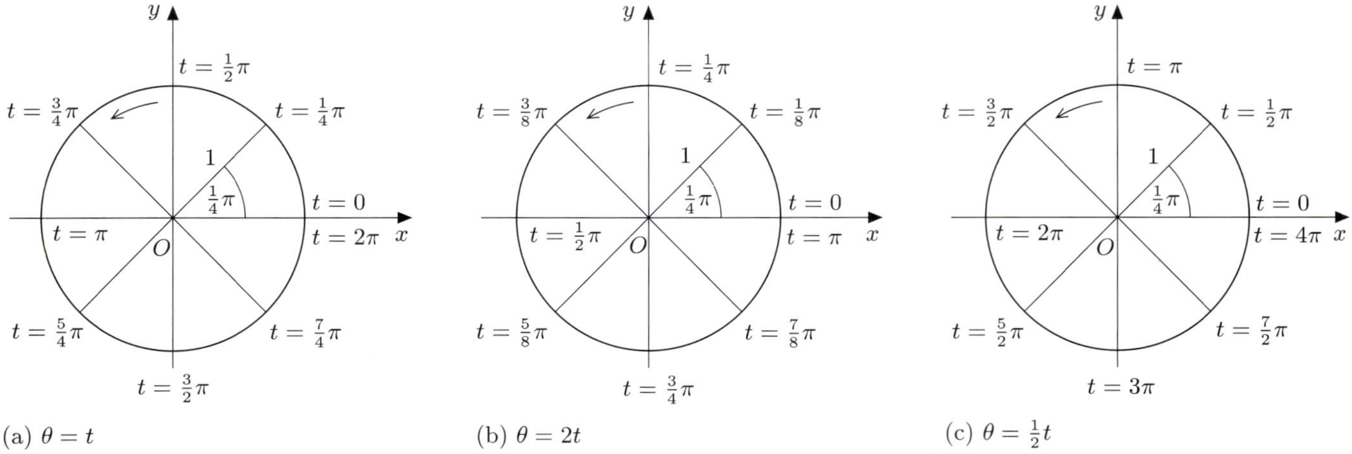

Figure 4.4 Three rates of motion

As shown, the motion is anticlockwise if k is positive. If k is negative (for example, $k = -1$ and $\theta = -t$), then the motion is in the clockwise direction around the circle.

Activity 4.4 Parametrisation for a given rate of motion

Find a parametrisation of the unit circle which corresponds to motion anticlockwise at the rate of one revolution per unit time.

A solution is given on page 57.

A parametrisation such as $x = \cos t$, $y = \sin t$ differs in an important respect from the parametrisations seen earlier for straight lines. The motion represented by the parametrisation here repeats itself every revolution (2π radians), since

$$\cos(t + 2\pi) = \cos t, \quad \sin(t + 2\pi) = \sin t.$$

Hence any single point on the circle corresponds to infinitely many values of t. If desired, this repetition can be avoided by placing a restriction on the values of t. For example, the equations

Even though $t = 0$ and $t = 2\pi$ give the same point, it is conventional to include both values in the range for t.

$$x = \cos t, \quad y = \sin t \quad (0 \leq t \leq 2\pi)$$

represent just one revolution around the unit circle, starting and finishing at $(x, y) = (\cos 0, \sin 0) = (1, 0)$. For other rates of motion around the circle, the restriction on t will need to be adjusted to achieve just one revolution. For example, the parametrisation

$$x = \cos(3t), \quad y = \sin(3t) \quad (0 \leq t \leq \tfrac{2}{3}\pi)$$

represents a complete turn around the circle at three times the previous rate, which is completed in one third of the time.

If less than the whole circle is to be described (a circular arc), then this can be achieved by specifying an even smaller range of values for t. For example,

$$x = \cos t, \quad y = \sin t \quad (0 \leq t \leq \pi)$$

is the upper unit semi-circle (see Figure 4.5(a)), whereas

Alternatively, the range for t for the lower semi-circle could be taken as $-\pi \leq t \leq 0$.

$$x = \cos t, \quad y = \sin t \quad (\pi \leq t \leq 2\pi)$$

is the lower unit semi-circle (Figure 4.5(b)).

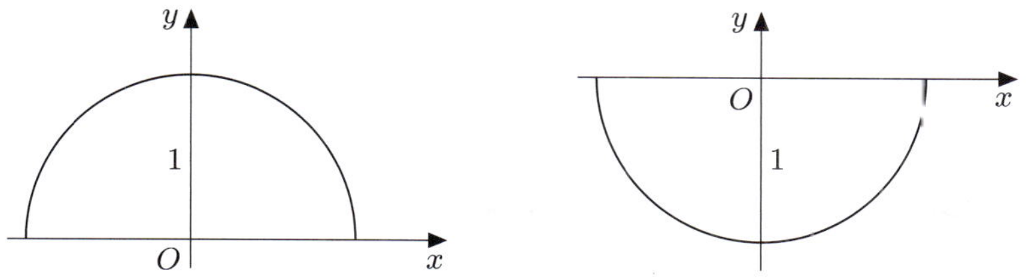

(a) $x = \cos t$, $y = \sin t$ for $0 \leq t \leq \pi$

(b) $x = \cos t$, $y = \sin t$ for $\pi \leq t \leq 2\pi$ (or, for $-\pi \leq t \leq 0$)

Figure 4.5 Two semi-circles

What has been said about parametrisations of the unit circle can be adapted readily to the case of any other circle. A circle with centre at (a, b) and radius r can be described by

$$x = a + r\cos\theta, \quad y = b + r\sin\theta,$$

and θ can be replaced by kt (where k is a non-zero constant) as before.

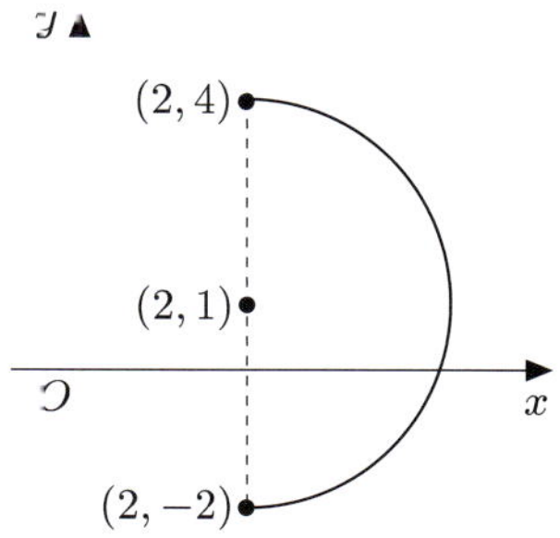

Figure 4.6 A semi-circle

Activity 4.5 Parametric equations for a semi-circle

Write down parametric equations, including an appropriate range for the parameter t, to describe the semi-circle shown in Figure 4.6.

A solution is given on page 57.

Summary of Section 4

This section has introduced:

- ◇ parametrisations for lines, and prescriptions for writing down parametric equations when the line is specified in terms of either (a) the slope of the line and 1 point on it, or (b) 2 points on the line;
- ◇ parametrisations for circles, and their connection with rate of motion around the circle if time is the parameter;
- ◇ the method for eliminating a parameter in order to obtain the equation for a line;
- ◇ the specification of part only of a line or circle, by placing appropriate restrictions on the parameter.

Exercises for Section 4

Exercise 4.1

(a) Write down parametric equations for the line which passes through the two points $(5, -2)$ and $(7, 4)$.

(b) Starting from your answer to part (a), deduce the equation of the line.

(c) Check that the coordinates of the two points given in part (a) satisfy the equation found in part (b).

Exercise 4.2

Write down parametric equations, including an appropriate range for the parameter t, for each of the following:

(a) the line segment joining the points $(-2, 4)$ and $(3, 1)$;

(b) the semi-circle shown in Figure 4.7.

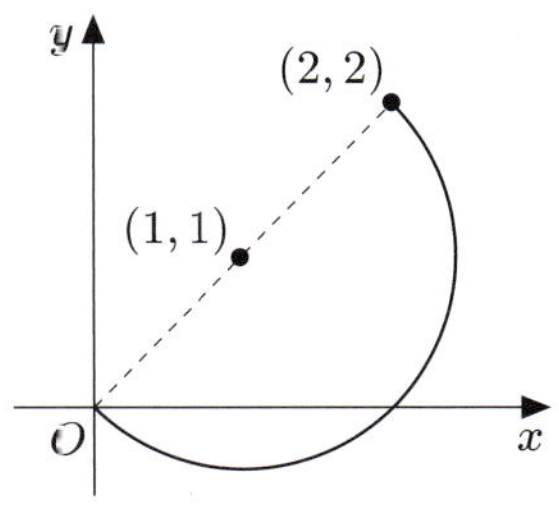

Figure 4.7 A semi-circle

5 Parametric equations by computer

To study this section you will need access to your computer, together with Computer Book A.

In this section you are invited to use your computer to plot lines and circles which are described by parametric equations. You will see also that the same approach can be adopted with other curves.

Refer to Computer Book A for the work in this section.

Summary of Section 5

This section has introduced:

◇ the approach needed to plot, by computer, a line, circle or other curve given by parametric equations.

Summary of Chapter A2

In this chapter you have studied the algebraic descriptions of lines and circles. These descriptions permit the solution of various problems stated initially in geometric rather than algebraic form. The links between geometry and algebra are of the greatest mathematical importance.

These links extend to the algebraic description of motion, which is provided by parametric equations for moving objects. Trigonometry provides useful parametrisations for circular motion.

Learning outcomes

You have been working towards the following learning outcomes.

Terms to know and use

Rectangular or Cartesian coordinates, axis, origin, rise and run, slope or gradient of a line, infinite slope, intercept, centre and radius of a circle, subtended angle, distance between two points, line segment, perpendicular bisector, midpoint, completing the square, completed-square form, unit circle, cosine, sine, degree, radian, quadrant, tangent, adjacent, opposite, hypotenuse, solving a triangle, parameter, parametrisation, parametric equations.

Symbols and notation to know and use

(x_1, y_1) for first point, (x_2, y_2) for second point, $\angle A$, $\triangle ABC$, $\sin\theta$, $\cos\theta$, $\tan\theta$, $\operatorname{cosec}\theta$, $\sec\theta$, $\cot\theta$, $\sin^2\theta$, etc., $0 \leq t \leq 1$.

Mathematical skills

- ◇ Obtain the equation of a line, either from its slope and one point on it, or from two points on it.
- ◇ Write down the slope of a line that is perpendicular to a line with given slope.
- ◇ Evaluate the distance between two points with given coordinates.
- ◇ Write down the equation of a circle with given centre and radius.
- ◇ Write down the coordinates of the midpoint of the line segment between two given points.
- ◇ Find the equation of the circle which passes through three given points, not all on the same straight line.
- ◇ Complete the square for a given expression of the form $x^2 + 2px$.
- ◇ Identify features of a line or circle from its equation.
- ◇ Find the point of intersection of two given non-parallel lines, or any points of intersection of a given line and circle, by solving the corresponding equations simultaneously.
- ◇ Use trigonometric ratios to solve right-angled triangles.
- ◇ Write down parametric equations for a given line or circle, or part thereof.
- ◇ From given parametric equations for a line, derive the corresponding non-parametric equation.

Mathcad skills

- ◇ Plot a curve which is specified by parametric equations.

Modelling skills

- ◇ Identify the variables in a situation, and find suitable equations to relate them.
- ◇ Appreciate that, in the process of mathematical modelling, doing the mathematics comes after creating the model and is followed by interpreting the results.

Ideas to be aware of

- ◇ Curves (including lines and circles) may be represented by algebraic equations.
- ◇ The slope of a line (the quantity 'rise $\div$ run') is a property which is independent of the two points on the line chosen to calculate the rise and run.
- ◇ The equation of a straight line is determined by its slope and one point on it, or alternatively by two points on it.
- ◇ The equation of a circle is determined by its radius and the position of its centre.
- ◇ Three points (not on the same straight line) determine a unique circle.
- ◇ The points which are equidistant from two given points, A and B, form the perpendicular bisector of the line segment AB.
- ◇ Sine and cosine can be seen as the components of steady circular motion.
- ◇ The slope of a line is equal to the tangent of the angle which it makes with the positive x-axis.
- ◇ A non-parametric equation describes a path, whereas parametric equations can describe the position at any given time of an object moving along that path.
- ◇ Completing the square permits the minimum or maximum value of a quadratic expression to be found.

Appendix: Modelling the Earth

This appendix contains a couple of illustrations of how the mathematics which has been introduced in this chapter can be applied in the real world. In each case, mathematical modelling is involved in translating a 'real problem' into mathematical terms, solving it and then interpreting the solution once more, though it is the mathematical ideas which we dwell most upon here.

The material in this appendix will not be assessed.

The first example concerns the basis of a major ground-surveying technique which predated the more sophisticated methods now available. Current ground surveys make substantial use of the satellite-based global positioning system described in the second example.

Applying trigonometry

Consider the problem of mapping a country. A basic requirement of a map is that it should represent to scale, with reasonable accuracy, the relative distances and orientations of all places of significance. One way of doing this is to divide the country up into a network of triangles. If the lengths of all sides of each triangle are measured, then its shape is also determined, so that we can represent it correctly to scale on a map.

As a simplifying assumption, the departures from flatness that occur on the surface of the Earth are ignored here, though it is important to take these into account when drawing an accurate map.

Drawbacks of this approach are the labour of carrying out all of the measurements, the problems posed in places by harsh terrain, and the difficulty, before the coming of photography and radar echo methods, of making length measurements on this scale accurately. These drawbacks were overcome during the eighteenth and early nineteenth centuries, by use of the theodolite (an instrument capable of measuring angles accurately) combined with application of the sine rule,

$$\frac{\sin A}{a} = \frac{\sin B}{b}.$$

The sine rule was introduced at the end of Section 3.

If the angles of a triangle and one of its sides have been measured, then the sine rule provides a simple way in which to calculate the lengths of the two remaining sides.

Suppose now that, in the network of triangles which covers the country, all the angles have been accurately recorded, and that the length of a single baseline, which is the side of one of the triangles, has also been measured (the side labelled 1 in Figure A.1).

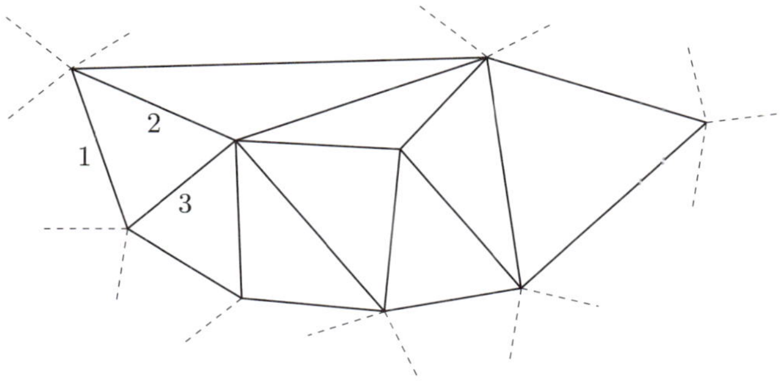

Figure A.1 Network of triangles

Then the lengths of the sides labelled 2 and 3 can be found by applying the sine rule. Once this has been done, we have two more known lengths on the diagram, so that other triangles which include these sides can be 'solved' in the same manner, by further applications of the sine rule. Continuing in this way, the lengths of all sides within the network can be obtained. Once the initial triangulation of a region is complete, more detail can be obtained using successively finer networks of smaller triangles.

The first national map to be based upon triangulation was the *Atlas National de France*. The work took place over the years 1733–1789. This map is also known as the 'Carte de Cassini', because the project involved four successive generations of the Cassini family.

The first local triangulations of this type took place in France in the late seventeenth century. The first Trigonometrical Survey (later called Ordnance Survey) of the British Isles was completed in 1873. It relied upon the accurate measurement (made in 1784) of a baseline of about 5 miles in length on Hounslow Heath.

Global positioning

Since July 1995, the Global Positioning System (GPS) developed and run by the United States Department of Defense has been fully operational. This system is available for civilian as well as for military purposes, and has already found wide applications for both commercial and leisure use. It enables users to establish their position in space (on the Earth's surface or above it) with considerable accuracy. However, the system is set up so that the fullest accuracy is available only to the US military.

The system has three components.

(a) Twenty-four satellites are maintained in high orbits above the Earth, each with an orbital period of 12 hours. Six separate planar orbits are used, with four satellites in each orbit. This configuration ensures that, with an unobstructed view skywards, a minimum of six satellites are always visible from any point on the Earth.

(b) Several ground stations around the world monitor the precise positions of the satellites, and also transmit information to them. These stations are linked to the centre of the operation at Colorado Springs.

(c) A receiver with built-in processor accompanies each user of the system. Receivers vary widely in sophistication: some types are hand-held and relatively cheap; others are built into ships or aircraft.

The system works as follows. The user's receiver 'locks onto' radio signals from several satellites. Assuming that a clock in the receiver is accurately synchronised with those in the satellites, the time lag between the transmission and reception of each signal can be measured. Since radio signals travel at the speed of light (about $300\,000\,\mathrm{km\,s^{-1}}$), the time lag measurements can be translated into distances. Each satellite transmits an accurate record of its own position at each moment, relative to a three-dimensional Cartesian coordinate system which is fixed relative to the Earth.

The receiver then has estimates of the distances to several satellites of known position at a particular time, and can calculate its own position at that time relative to the same coordinate system. This can then be translated, if desired, into the longitude, latitude and altitude of the receiver. Repeated calculations of this type can also tell the user what their speed and direction of motion are.

To understand how the position of the receiver can be derived from the calculated distances from the satellites, let us simplify matters by considering the corresponding situation in two space dimensions rather than the original three.

Figure A.2 shows the position of the user at a point P relative to two transmitting devices (corresponding to satellites) at points A and B. The coordinates of A and B are known, relative to a fixed origin at O and Cartesian (x, y)-axes.

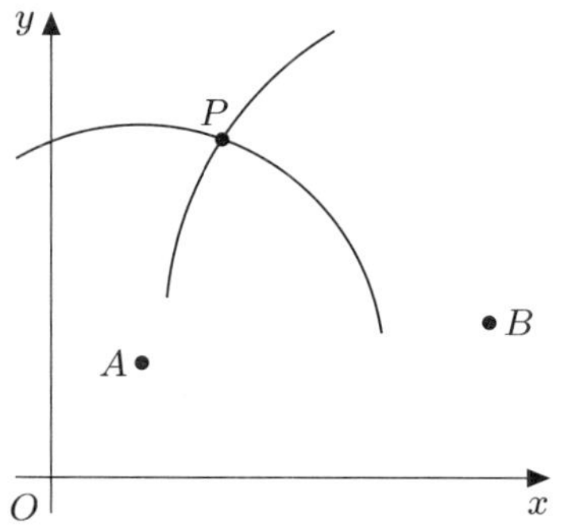

Figure A.2 Points A, B and P

The point P is at the intersection of two circles, with centres at A and at B. The coordinates of these centres are known, and so are the radii (the distances from the transmitters), so that in each case we can write down an equation for the circle. Finding the position of P therefore amounts to finding a point where the two circles intersect. The mathematics needed to locate these intersection points was discussed at the end of Subsection 2.4.

In fact, there will be two such intersection points, but in practice it will be possible to discount one as giving an 'absurd' result.

Hence measurements from just two transmitters should suffice to fix the position of the user in our simplified two-dimensional situation. This generalises in a straightforward manner to three space dimensions, with the circles replaced by spheres. Measurements from three satellites fix the position of the user. The equations involved look more complicated than those for circles, but they can be solved simultaneously for the intersection point in a very similar way. However, there is a snag!

It was assumed, at the start of describing how the system works, that the clock in the receiver was accurately synchronised with those in the satellites. The satellites do indeed incorporate highly accurate clocks. Receivers, on the other hand, would be prohibitively expensive if they had clocks of comparable accuracy. Therefore their timing devices, although good by everyday standards, are not adequately accurate for the purpose described here. To appreciate what is involved, note that with the transmitted signals travelling at the speed of light, a timing error of a millisecond corresponds to a distance error of 300 km!

Luckily, there is a simple way around this problem, which is to *use data from an additional satellite.* To see how this works in terms of our two-dimensional situation, look at Figure A.3.

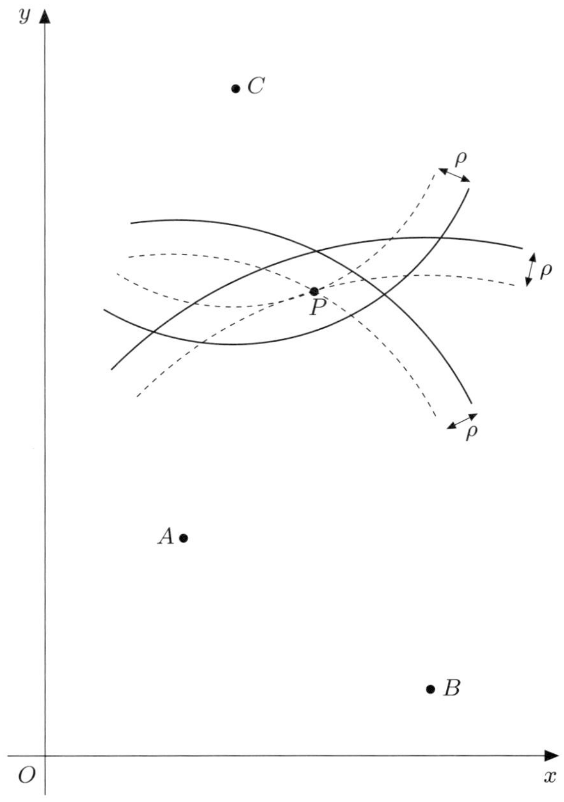

Figure A.3 Effects of time error in receiver

As before, there are transmitters at known positions A and B, but there is also a third transmitter at position C. If the receiver's clock were accurate, then the three calculated distances would be equal to the radii of three circles which intersect at a single point. Due to time error in the receiver, this does not occur. Instead, the calculated distances lead to the circles shown solid in Figure A.3, which do *not* intersect mutually at a point. This shows up the time error in the receiver. Since these calculations are clearly inaccurate, the three distances are called *pseudoranges* from the transmitters.

The symbols τ and ρ are the Greek letters 'tau' and 'rho', respectively.

The saving grace here is that the time error is the same for each of the three time measurements. Hence we may seek a value of τ, the time error, such that removing a distance $\rho = c\tau$ (where c is the speed of light) from each pseudorange will produce three circles which *do* intersect in a single point (the broken circles in Figure A.3). This intersection point is the position P of the user. As a by-product, the value found for τ is the receiver's time error, which can be used to correct the time registered by the receiver.

The user then has a calculated time which is as accurate as that on the satellites!

Hence it takes three transmitters to locate accurately in two space dimensions a receiver with a slightly inaccurate clock. In three space dimensions, a similar approach succeeds with data from four satellites.

Solutions to Activities

Solution 1.1

(a) Any point on the line parallel to and 3 units to the left of the y-axis has coordinates of the form $(-3, y)$, so these coordinates satisfy the condition $x = -3$. This is therefore the required equation of the line.

(b) In general, any line parallel to the y-axis has an equation of the form $x = d$, where d is a constant. The value of d is negative for a line to the left of the y-axis, and positive for a line to the right.

(c)

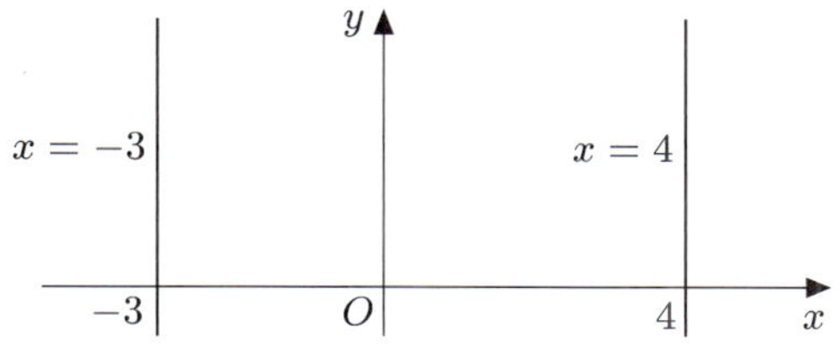

Figure S.1

Solution 1.2

(a) If the run is zero, then $x_1 = x_2$. One of the points is vertically above the other, so the line is parallel to the y-axis. Although the slope is not then defined by the expression 'rise ÷ run', we say that such a line has *infinite slope*.
(As you found in Activity 1.1, such a line has an equation of the form $x = d$, where d is a constant. Here $x_1 = x_2 = d$.)

(b) If the slope is zero, then the rise $y_2 - y_1$ must be zero, so $y_2 = y_1$. Both points are at the same horizontal level, so the line is parallel to the x-axis. (As pointed out earlier, such a line has an equation of the form $y = c$, where c is a constant. Here $y_1 = y_2 = c$.)

Solution 1.3

The four lines are sketched in Figure S.2. (It is not necessary to sketch all the lines on the same axes.)

In the equation $y = mx + c$, the value of c is the y-intercept, and the value of m is the slope. Hence the first two lines pass through the origin. The slope information may be used by recalling that the slope is 'rise ÷ run', so that a run of 1 (say) will correspond to a rise equal to the value of the slope. This approach can be used to derive a second point through which the line passes (as well as $(0, c)$). For example, the line $y = \frac{1}{3}x$ passes through $(1, \frac{1}{3})$ as well as through the origin. Similarly, the line $y = -3x + 1$ passes through $(0, 1)$, but also, with a run of 1, through

$$(1, -3 \times 1 + 1) = (1, -2).$$

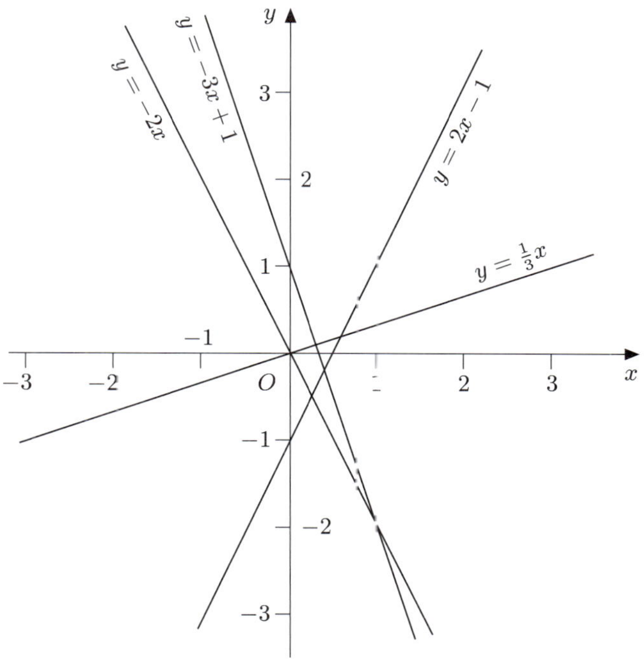

Figure S.2

Solution 1.4

(a) The equation of the line has the form $y - y_1 = m(x - x_1)$, where the slope is $m = -2$ and the line passes through the point $(x_1, y_1) = (5, -3)$. Hence the equation is

$$y - (-3) = -2(x - 5).$$

On multiplying out the brackets and then subtracting 3 from both sides, this becomes

$$y = -2x + 7.$$

(b) From $(0, -6)$ to $(3, 0)$, the run is $3 - 0 = 3$ and the rise is $0 - (-6) = 6$. Hence the slope m is given by

$$m = \tfrac{6}{3} = 2.$$

Since the y-intercept -6 is given, the $y = mx + c$ form of the equation of a line can be applied directly, with $c = -6$. The equation of the given line is therefore

$$y = 2x - 6.$$

As a check, the pair of values $x = 3$, $y = 0$ satisfies this equation, verifying that the point $(3, 0)$ lies on the line.

Solution 1.5

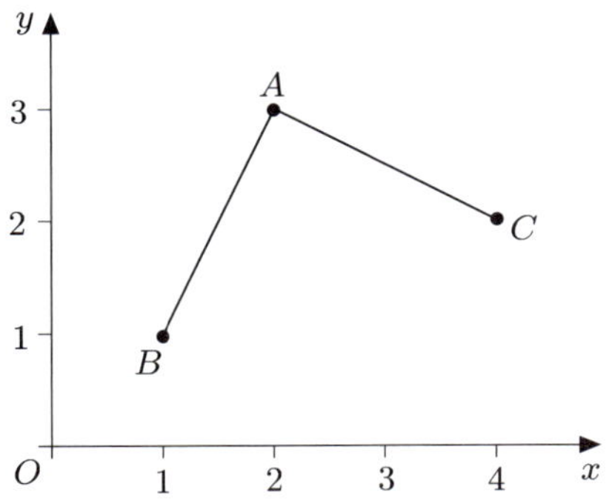

Figure S.3

The slope of AB is $\dfrac{1-3}{1-2} = \dfrac{-2}{-1} = 2.$

The slope of AC is $\dfrac{2-3}{4-2} = \dfrac{-1}{2} = -\dfrac{1}{2}.$

Solution 1.6

(a) From $A(-1,4)$ to $B(5,2)$, the run is $5-(-1)=6$ and the rise is $2-4=-2$. Hence the slope of AB is $-2 \div 6 = -\frac{1}{3}$.

(b) Each line which is perpendicular to AB has slope $-1/(-\frac{1}{3}) = 3$.

(c) The required line has slope 3, and hence has an equation of the form $y - y_1 = 3(x - x_1)$. Now the point $A(-1,4)$ is to lie on this line, so put $(x_1, y_1) = (-1, 4)$. This gives

$$y - 4 = 3(x - (-1));$$

that is,

$$y = 3x + 7.$$

Solution 1.7

(a) The lines $y = 5x - 7$ and $y = -3x + 1$ meet where

$$5x - 7 = -3x + 1; \quad \text{that is,} \quad x = 1.$$

The corresponding y-coordinate is $y = 5 \times 1 - 7 = -2$. Hence the point of intersection of the two lines has coordinates $(1, -2)$. (These coordinates also satisfy the second equation, as you should have checked!)

(b) Attempting to follow the same approach with the two lines $y = 2x + 3$ and $y = 2x - 3$, we obtain

$$2x + 3 = 2x - 3; \quad \text{that is,} \quad 3 = -3!$$

This is clearly untrue, and indicates that no solution (x, y) can be found which satisfies the two equations simultaneously. Geometrically speaking, there is a simple explanation for this: the two lines are parallel (each has slope 2) and hence never meet.

Solution 1.8

(a) The passenger train travels at 100 km per hour, and starts at $t = 0$ (7 am). Hence its equation is

$$d = 100t.$$

(b) The freight train starts at 8.30 am, which is at $t = 1.5$. Its distance from Edinburgh is then $d = 600$. Hence at 8.30 am we have $(t, d) = (1.5, 600)$.

Since the freight train travels *towards* Edinburgh at 60 km per hour, its equation has the form $d = -60t + c$. From $(t, d) = (1.5, 600)$, we obtain

$$600 = -60 \times 1.5 + c; \quad \text{that is,} \quad c = 690.$$

So the equation for the freight train is

$$d = -60t + 690.$$

(c) The graphs are shown below. They indicate that the two trains pass each other between $t = 4$ and $t = 4.5$, that is, between 11 am and 11.30 am. At this time, they are about 430 km from Edinburgh.

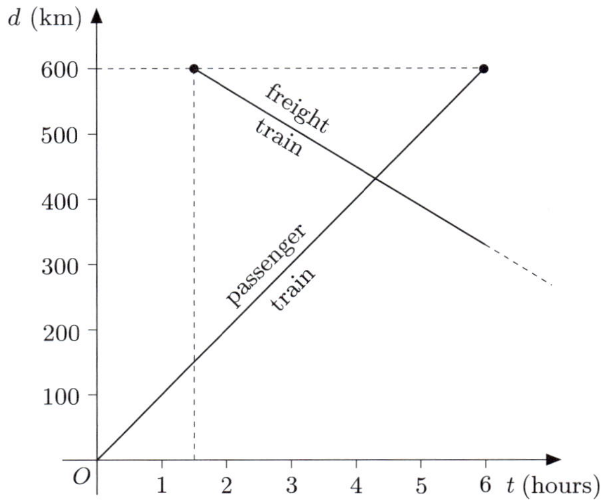

Figure S.4

(d) The two trains meet when the equations $d = 100t$ and $d = -60t + 690$ are satisfied simultaneously. This occurs when

$$100t = -60t + 690; \quad \text{that is,} \quad t = \tfrac{69}{16} = 4.3125.$$

The corresponding value of d is

$$d = 100 \times 4.3125 = 431.25.$$

Now 0.3125 hours is $60 \times 0.3125 = 18.75$ minutes. Hence the two trains pass when about 431 km away from Edinburgh and at about 11.19 am. These results agree with the graphical ones from part (c).

Solution 2.2

(a) The square of the distance between the points $(3, 2)$ and $(7, 5)$ is

$$(7-3)^2 + (5-2)^2 = 4^2 + 3^2 = 25.$$

Hence the distance is $\sqrt{25} = 5$.

(b) The square of the distance between the points $(-1, 4)$ and $(3, -2)$ is

$$(3-(-1))^2 + (-2-4)^2 = 4^2 + (-6)^2 = 52.$$

Hence the distance is $\sqrt{52} = 2\sqrt{13} \simeq 7.21$.

Solution 2.3

(a) Centre at $(0, 0)$, radius 3: equation is $x^2 + y^2 = 9$.

(b) Centre at $(5, 7)$, radius $\sqrt{2}$: equation is $(x-5)^2 + (y-7)^2 = 2\ (= (\sqrt{2})^2)$.

(c) Centre at $(-3, -1)$, radius 1: equation is $(x-(-3))^2 + (y-(-1))^2 = 1$; that is, $(x+3)^2 + (y+1)^2 = 1$.

Solution 2.4

(a) $(x-1)^2 + (y-2)^2 = 25$: centre is at $(1, 2)$, radius is 5 $(= \sqrt{25}\,)$.

(b) $(x+1)^2 + (y+2)^2 = 49$: centre is at $(-1, -2)$, radius is 7.

(c) $(x-\pi)^2 + (y+\pi)^2 = \pi^2$: centre is at $(\pi, -\pi)$, radius is π.

(d) $x^2 + (y-\sqrt{3}\,)^2 = 7$: centre is at $(0, \sqrt{3}\,)$, radius is $\sqrt{7}$.

Solution 2.5

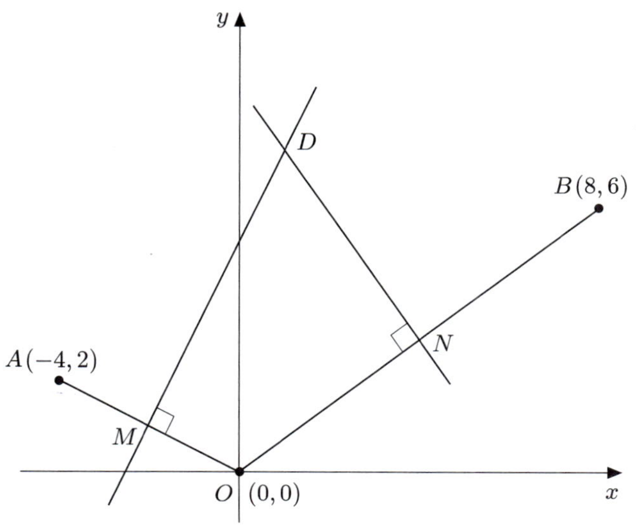

Figure S.5

(a) The line segment OA has slope $(2-0) \div (-4-0) = -\frac{1}{2}$ and midpoint M at $(\frac{1}{2}(-4+0), \frac{1}{2}(2+0)) = (-2, 1)$. Its perpendicular bisector MD therefore has slope 2 (using the perpendicularity condition from Subsection 1.1) and passes through $(-2, 1)$. Its equation is

$$y - 1 = 2(x-(-2)); \quad \text{that is,} \quad y = 2x + 5.$$

(b) Similarly, the line segment OB has slope $(6-0) \div (8-0) = \frac{3}{4}$ and midpoint N at $(\frac{1}{2}(8+0), \frac{1}{2}(6+0)) = (4, 3)$. Its perpendicular bisector ND therefore has slope $-\frac{4}{3}$ and passes through $(4, 3)$. Its equation is

$$y - 3 = -\tfrac{4}{3}(x-4); \quad \text{that is,} \quad y = -\tfrac{4}{3}x + \tfrac{25}{3}.$$

(c) The two perpendicular bisectors, $y = 2x + 5$ (MD) and $y = -\frac{4}{3}x + \frac{25}{3}$ (ND), intersect at D, where

$$2x + 5 = -\tfrac{4}{3}x + \tfrac{25}{3}; \quad \text{that is,} \quad x = 1.$$

By substituting this value of x into the equation for MD, we find that the corresponding value of y is $y = 2 \times 1 + 5 = 7$, so the centre D of the circle is at $(1, 7)$.

(d) The radius r is the distance between D and O (or A, or B), so it is given by

$$r^2 = (1-0)^2 + (7-0)^2 = 50;$$

thus the radius is $r = \sqrt{50} = 5\sqrt{2} \simeq 7.07$.

(e) The equation of the circle is

$$(x-1)^2 + (y-7)^2 = 50.$$

Solution 2.6

(a) Comparing $x^2 - 4x$ with the identity

$$x^2 + 2px = (x+p)^2 - p^2,$$

we can match the left-hand sides by putting $2p = -4$; that is, $p = -2$. Putting this value also into the right-hand side, we obtain the completed-square form

$$x^2 - 4x = (x-2)^2 - (-2)^2 = (x-2)^2 - 4.$$

(b) Comparing $y^2 - 6y$ with the general form

$$y^2 + 2py = (y+p)^2 - p^2,$$

we can match the left-hand sides by putting $2p = -6$; that is, $p = -3$. Putting this value also into the right-hand side, we obtain the completed-square form

$$y^2 - 6y = (y-3)^2 - (-3)^2 = (y-3)^2 - 9.$$

(c) Now substitute both of the completed-square forms into the equation given, namely

$$x^2 - 4x + y^2 - 6y - 12 = 0.$$

In terms of the completed-square forms, this becomes

$$(x-2)^2 - 4 + (y-3)^2 - 9 - 12 = 0.$$

On collecting the number terms and rearranging, we have

$$(x-2)^2 + (y-3)^2 = 25 = 5^2.$$

Hence the equation is indeed that of a circle, which has centre $(2,3)$ and radius 5.

Solution 2.7

Using the equation of the line, $y = x + 2$, to substitute for y in the equation of the circle, $(x-3)^2 + (y+4)^2 = 53$, we have

$$(x-3)^2 + (x+2+4)^2 = 53.$$

On multiplying out the brackets and simplifying, we obtain the successive equations

$$(x-3)^2 + (x+6)^2 = 53,$$
$$x^2 - 6x + 9 + x^2 + 12x + 36 = 53,$$
$$2x^2 + 6x - 8 = 0,$$
$$x^2 + 3x - 4 = 0.$$

The last equation factorises as $(x+4)(x-1) = 0$, from which the solutions are $x = -4$ and $x = 1$. Using each of these values in turn in the equation of the line, we obtain, respectively, $y = -4 + 2 = -2$ and $y = 1 + 2 = 3$.

The line cuts the circle at the two points $(-4,-2)$ and $(1,3)$.

Solution 3.1

For θ equal to 0, $-\frac{1}{2}\pi$ and π, the corresponding positions of $P(x,y)$ on the unit circle are $(1,0)$, $(0,-1)$ and $(-1,0)$. The solutions below are then obtained by applying the definitions $\cos\theta = x$ and $\sin\theta = y$.

(a) $\cos 0 = 1$ and $\sin 0 = 0$

(b) $\cos(-\frac{1}{2}\pi) = 0$ and $\sin(-\frac{1}{2}\pi) = -1$

(c) $\cos\pi = -1$ and $\sin\pi = 0$

Solution 3.2

(a) From the formula $\cos(\frac{1}{2}\pi - \theta) = \sin\theta$, we have $\cos(\frac{1}{2}\pi - \frac{1}{4}\pi) = \sin(\frac{1}{4}\pi)$; that is,

$$\cos(\tfrac{1}{4}\pi) = \sin(\tfrac{1}{4}\pi).$$

Also,

$$\cos^2(\tfrac{1}{4}\pi) + \sin^2(\tfrac{1}{4}\pi) = 1.$$

Hence we have $2\cos^2(\frac{1}{4}\pi) = 1$; that is, $\cos^2(\frac{1}{4}\pi) = \frac{1}{2}$. We conclude that

$$\cos(\tfrac{1}{4}\pi) = \sin(\tfrac{1}{4}\pi) = \tfrac{1}{2}\sqrt{2}.$$

We choose the positive square root here because the angle lies in the first quadrant, and hence its sine and cosine are both positive (see Figure 3.2).

(b) Each angle of an equilateral triangle is $\frac{1}{3}\pi$ (60°), so $\theta = \frac{1}{6}\pi$. The side PQ of the triangle has length 1 (equal to the other two sides), and since the x-axis bisects this side, the y-coordinate of P is $\frac{1}{2}$. It follows that $\sin(\frac{1}{6}\pi) = \frac{1}{2}$.

We also have $\cos^2(\frac{1}{6}\pi) + \sin^2(\frac{1}{6}\pi) = 1$, from which

$$\cos^2(\tfrac{1}{6}\pi) = 1 - \sin^2(\tfrac{1}{6}\pi) = 1 - (\tfrac{1}{2})^2 = \tfrac{3}{4}.$$

Hence, since $\cos(\frac{1}{6}\pi)$ is positive, we obtain

$$\cos(\tfrac{1}{6}\pi) = \tfrac{1}{2}\sqrt{3}.$$

(c) Using the formulas

$$\cos(\tfrac{1}{2}\pi - \theta) = \sin\theta, \quad \sin(\tfrac{1}{2}\pi - \theta) = \cos\theta,$$

together with the results from part (b), we have

$$\cos(\tfrac{1}{3}\pi) = \sin(\tfrac{1}{6}\pi) = \tfrac{1}{2},$$
$$\sin(\tfrac{1}{3}\pi) = \cos(\tfrac{1}{6}\pi) = \tfrac{1}{2}\sqrt{3}.$$

Solution 3.3

Apply the definition $\tan\theta = \sin\theta/(\cos\theta)$, and use the values of cos and sin of angles found in Activities 3.1 and 3.2, to obtain the following.

(a) $\tan 0 = \dfrac{\sin 0}{\cos 0} = \dfrac{0}{1} = 0$

(b) $\tan\pi = \dfrac{\sin\pi}{\cos\pi} = \dfrac{0}{-1} = 0$

(c) $\tan(\frac{1}{4}\pi) = \dfrac{\sin(\frac{1}{4}\pi)}{\cos(\frac{1}{4}\pi)} = \dfrac{\frac{1}{2}\sqrt{2}}{\frac{1}{2}\sqrt{2}} = 1$

(d) $\tan(\frac{1}{6}\pi) = \dfrac{\sin(\frac{1}{6}\pi)}{\cos(\frac{1}{6}\pi)} = \dfrac{\frac{1}{2}}{\frac{1}{2}\sqrt{3}} = \dfrac{1}{\sqrt{3}} = \frac{1}{3}\sqrt{3}$

(e) $\tan(\frac{1}{3}\pi) = \dfrac{\sin(\frac{1}{3}\pi)}{\cos(\frac{1}{3}\pi)} = \dfrac{\frac{1}{2}\sqrt{3}}{\frac{1}{2}} = \sqrt{3}$

Solution 3.4

(a) $\sin(\frac{5}{6}\pi) = \sin(\pi - \frac{1}{6}\pi) = \sin(\frac{1}{6}\pi) = \frac{1}{2}$

(b) $\cos(\frac{5}{6}\pi) = \cos(\pi - \frac{1}{6}\pi) = -\cos(\frac{1}{6}\pi) = -\frac{1}{2}\sqrt{3}$

(c) $\tan(\frac{2}{3}\pi) = \tan(\pi - \frac{1}{3}\pi) = -\tan(\frac{1}{3}\pi) = -\sqrt{3}$

(d) $\tan(-\frac{1}{3}\pi) = -\tan(\frac{1}{3}\pi) = -\sqrt{3}$

Solution 3.5

In each case, there are many valid approaches.

In this solution and in similar situations, it is convenient to use the symbol $\angle$, which is read as 'angle'.

(a) Since $AB = 22$ and $\angle B = 47°$, we have $\angle A = 90° - 47° = 43°$. Then, using the definitions of sine and cosine,

$$AC = 22 \sin 47° \simeq 16.1,$$
$$BC = 22 \cos 47° \simeq 15.0.$$

(b) By Pythagoras' Theorem, we have $AC^2 = 22^2 - 13^2 = 315$, so

$$AC = \sqrt{315} \simeq 17.7.$$

The cosine of $\angle B$ is $\frac{13}{22}$. Applying the 'inverse cosine' facility on a calculator gives the result $\angle B \simeq 53.8°$. Then the remaining angle is given by $\angle A = 90° - \angle B \simeq 36.2°$.

Solution 4.1

(a) The line has slope $m = 3$ and passes through $(x_1, y_1) = (1, -2)$. Hence the parametric equation expressions

$$x = t + x_1, \quad y = mt + y_1$$

lead to

$$x = t + 1, \quad y = 3t - 2.$$

(b) The line passes through $(x_1, y_1) = (1, 5)$ and $(x_2, y_2) = (4, -7)$. Hence the parametric equation expressions

$$x = x_1 + t(x_2 - x_1), \quad y = y_1 + t(y_2 - y_1)$$

lead to

$$x = 3t + 1, \quad y = -12t + 5.$$

(Note that if the points had been taken in the other order, the parametric equations would have been

$$x = -3t + 4, \quad y = 12t - 7.)$$

Solution 4.2

If $x = 3t + 1$, then $t = \frac{1}{3}(x - 1)$. Hence we have

$$y = -12t + 5 = -12 \times \tfrac{1}{3}(x - 1) + 5 = -4x + 9;$$

that is, the equation of the line is $y = -4x + 9$.

(The parametric equations given here are those found in Solution 4.1(b). You might like to check that the alternative parametric equation expressions

$$x = -3t + 4, \quad y = 12t - 7$$

also lead to the equation

$$y = -4x + 9.)$$

Solution 4.3

At time t, the distance d between the two aircraft is given by

$$\begin{aligned} d^2 &= \left(500t + 10 - (496t + 22)\right)^2 \\ &\quad + \left(-312t - 12 - (-310t - 23)\right)^2 \\ &= (4t - 12)^2 + (-2t + 11)^2 \\ &= 16t^2 - 96t + 144 + 4t^2 - 44t + 121 \\ &= 20t^2 - 140t + 265 \\ &= 20(t^2 - 7t) + 265. \end{aligned}$$

Applying the 'completing the square' formula to the expression in brackets gives

$$d^2 = 20\left((t - \tfrac{7}{2})^2 - \tfrac{49}{4}\right) + 265 = 20\left(t - \tfrac{7}{2}\right)^2 + 20.$$

The term $20(t - \frac{7}{2})^2$ never takes a value less than 0, and it achieves the value 0 when $t = \frac{7}{2}$. At this time, the value of d^2 is 20. Hence the closest approach distance is $\sqrt{20} \simeq 4.47$ (km), and this occurs when $t = 3.5$ (hours).

Solution 4.4

We seek equations of the form $x = \cos\theta$, $y = \sin\theta$, with $\theta = kt$ and $k > 0$ (for anticlockwise motion). In one revolution, θ increases by 2π (radians), and hence t increases by $2\pi/k$. If this is to take place in unit time, then $2\pi/k = 1$, that is, $k = 2\pi$. Possible equations to meet the prescription given are therefore

$$x = \cos(2\pi t), \quad y = \sin(2\pi t).$$

Solution 4.5

The semi-circle has centre $(a, b) = (2, 1)$ and radius $r = 3$. Putting also $k = 1$ in the general equations

$$x = a + r\cos(kt), \quad y = b + r\sin(kt),$$

we have the parametric equations

$$x = 2 + 3\cos t, \quad y = 1 + 3\sin t.$$

Without any restriction on t, these equations describe a circle. In order to describe the semi-circle shown, an appropriate range for t is $-\frac{1}{2}\pi \le t \le \frac{1}{2}\pi$. (There are other ranges which will do equally well, for example, $\frac{3}{2}\pi \le t \le \frac{5}{2}\pi$.)

Solutions to Exercises

Solution 1.1

(a) The rise from $(3, 2)$ to $(-1, 10)$ is $10 - 2 = 8$. The run is $-1 - 3 = -4$.

(b) The slope of the line is

$$\frac{\text{rise}}{\text{run}} = \frac{8}{-4} = -2.$$

(c) Apply the general formula of a line in the form $y - y_1 = m(x - x_1)$, with slope $m = -2$ and $(x_1, y_1) = (3, 2)$. This gives

$$y - 2 = -2(x - 3); \quad \text{that is,} \quad y = -2x + 8.$$

As a check, $x = -1$ and $y = 10$ satisfy this equation (the point $(-1, 10)$ lies on the line).

(d) The x-intercept is the value of x when $y = 0$, which is the solution of $-2x + 8 = 0$. Hence the x-intercept is 4. The y-intercept is 8 (the value of y when $x = 0$).

Solution 1.2

From $(2, 3)$ to $(-1, -2)$, the rise is $-2 - 3 = -5$ and the run is $-1 - 2 = -3$, so the slope of the line is $\frac{5}{3}$. Since the line passes through the point $(2, 3)$, its equation can be written as

$$y - 3 = \tfrac{5}{3}(x - 2),$$

which can be rearranged as $y = \frac{5}{3}x - \frac{1}{3}$.

Solution 1.3

The line found in Exercise 1.2 has slope $\frac{5}{3}$, so the slope of each line perpendicular to it has slope $-1/(\frac{5}{3}) = -\frac{3}{5}$. The required line also passes through the point $(2, 3)$, so its equation can be written as

$$y - 3 = -\tfrac{3}{5}(x - 2).$$

This can be rearranged as $y = -\frac{3}{5}x + \frac{21}{5}$.

Solution 1.4

The two lines $y = 5x - 7$ and $y = -x + 11$ meet when

$$5x - 7 = -x + 11; \quad \text{that is,} \quad x = 3.$$

The corresponding value of y is $y = 5 \times 3 - 7 = 8$, so the lines intersect at the point $(3, 8)$.

Solution 2.1

(a) The circle with centre $(2, 3)$ and radius 4 has equation

$$(x - 2)^2 + (y - 3)^2 = 16.$$

(b) The circle with equation $(x + 5)^2 + (y - 4)^2 = 17$ has centre $(-5, 4)$ and radius $\sqrt{17}$.

Solution 2.2

The line segment AB has slope $(0 - 2) \div (-1 - (-2)) = -2$ and midpoint $(\frac{1}{2}(-2 - 1), \frac{1}{2}(2 + 0)) = (-\frac{3}{2}, 1)$. Its perpendicular bisector therefore has slope $\frac{1}{2}$ (using the perpendicularity condition from Subsection 1.1) and passes through $(-\frac{3}{2}, 1)$, so its equation is

$$y - 1 = \tfrac{1}{2}(x - (-\tfrac{3}{2})); \quad \text{that is,} \quad y = \tfrac{1}{2}x + \tfrac{7}{4}.$$

Similarly, the line segment BC has slope $(6 - 0) \div (1 - (-1)) = 3$ and midpoint $(\frac{1}{2}(-1 + 1), \frac{1}{2}(0 + 6)) = (0, 3)$. Its perpendicular bisector therefore has slope $-\frac{1}{3}$ and passes through $(0, 3)$, so its equation is

$$y - 3 = -\tfrac{1}{3}(x - 0); \quad \text{that is,} \quad y = -\tfrac{1}{3}x + 3.$$

The two perpendicular bisectors, $y = \frac{1}{2}x + \frac{7}{4}$ and $y = -\frac{1}{3}x + 3$, intersect where

$$\tfrac{1}{2}x + \tfrac{7}{4} = -\tfrac{1}{3}x + 3; \quad \text{that is,} \quad x = \tfrac{3}{2}.$$

The corresponding value of y is $y = \frac{1}{2} \times \frac{3}{2} + \frac{7}{4} = \frac{5}{2}$, so the centre D of the circle is at $(\frac{3}{2}, \frac{5}{2})$.

The radius r is the distance between D and B (or A, or C), so it is given by

$$r^2 = (\tfrac{3}{2} - (-1))^2 + (\tfrac{5}{2} - 0)^2 = \tfrac{50}{4} = \tfrac{25}{2}.$$

The radius is $r = \frac{5}{2}\sqrt{2} \simeq 3.54$.

The equation of the circle is

$$(x - \tfrac{3}{2})^2 + (y - \tfrac{5}{2})^2 = \tfrac{25}{2}.$$

Solution 2.3

(a) Comparing $x^2 + 14x$ with the identity

$$x^2 + 2px = (x + p)^2 - p^2$$

from Subsection 2.3, we can match the left-hand side by putting $2p = 14$; that is, $p = 7$. Putting this value also into the right-hand side, we obtain the completed-square form

$$x^2 + 14x = (x + 7)^2 - 7^2 = (x + 7)^2 - 49.$$

(b) Comparing $y^2 - 24y$ with the general form

$$y^2 + 2py = (y + p)^2 - p^2,$$

we can match the left-hand side by putting $2p = -24$; that is, $p = -12$. Putting this value also into the right-hand side, we obtain the completed-square form

$$\begin{aligned} y^2 - 24y &= (y - 12)^2 - (-12)^2 \\ &= (y - 12)^2 - 144. \end{aligned}$$

(c) The equation given is

$$x^2 + 14x + y^2 - 24y - 96 = 0.$$

In terms of the completed-square forms, this becomes

$$(x + 7)^2 - 49 + (y - 12)^2 - 144 - 96 = 0.$$

On collecting the number terms and rearranging, we have

$$(x + 7)^2 + (y - 12)^2 = 289 = 17^2.$$

Hence the equation is indeed that of a circle, which has centre at $(-7, 12)$ and radius 17.

Solution 2.4

Using the equation of the line, $y = \frac{3}{2}x + \frac{3}{2}$, to substitute for y in the equation of the circle, $(x - 3)^2 + (y + 7)^2 = 65$, we have

$$(x - 3)^2 + (\tfrac{3}{2}x + \tfrac{3}{2} + 7)^2 = 65.$$

On multiplying out the brackets and simplifying, we obtain the successive equations

$$\begin{aligned}
&(x - 3)^2 + (\tfrac{3}{2}x + \tfrac{17}{2})^2 = 65,\\
&(x - 3)^2 + (\tfrac{1}{2})^2(3x + 17)^2 = 65,\\
&4(x - 3)^2 + (3x + 17)^2 = 260,\\
&4(x^2 - 6x + 9) + 9x^2 + 102x + 289 = 260,\\
&13x^2 + 78x + 65 = 0,\\
&x^2 + 6x + 5 = 0.
\end{aligned}$$

The last equation factorises as $(x + 5)(x + 1) = 0$, from which the solutions are $x = -5$ and $x = -1$. Using each of these values in turn in the equation of the line, we obtain, respectively, $y = \frac{3}{2} \times (-5) + \frac{3}{2} = -6$ and $y = \frac{3}{2} \times (-1) + \frac{3}{2} = 0$.

The line cuts the circle at the two points $(-5, -6)$ and $(-1, 0)$.

Solution 3.1

(a) On replacing θ by $-\theta$ in the formulas

$$\cos(\pi - \theta) = -\cos\theta, \quad \sin(\pi - \theta) = \sin\theta,$$

we have

$$\begin{aligned}
\cos(\theta + \pi) &= -\cos(-\theta),\\
\sin(\theta + \pi) &= \sin(-\theta).
\end{aligned}$$

Now apply the further formulas

$$\cos(-\theta) = \cos\theta, \quad \sin(-\theta) = -\sin\theta,$$

to obtain the results

$$\cos(\theta + \pi) = -\cos\theta, \quad \sin(\theta + \pi) = -\sin\theta.$$

(b) (i) $\sin(\frac{7}{6}\pi) = \sin(\frac{1}{6}\pi + \pi) = -\sin(\frac{1}{6}\pi) = -\frac{1}{2}$

(ii) $\cos(\frac{7}{6}\pi) = \cos(\frac{1}{6}\pi + \pi) = -\cos(\frac{1}{6}\pi) = -\frac{1}{2}\sqrt{3}$

(iii) $\tan(\frac{7}{6}\pi) = \dfrac{\sin(\frac{7}{6}\pi)}{\cos(\frac{7}{6}\pi)} = \dfrac{-\frac{1}{2}}{-\frac{1}{2}\sqrt{3}} = \dfrac{1}{\sqrt{3}} = \frac{1}{3}\sqrt{3}$

Solution 3.2

In each case, there are many valid approaches.

(a) Since $AC = 7$ and $\angle B = 35°$, we have

$$\begin{aligned}
\angle A &= 90° - 35° = 55°,\\
BC &= 7\tan 55° \simeq 10.0,\\
AB &= \frac{7}{\sin 35°} \simeq 12.2.
\end{aligned}$$

(b) By Pythagoras' Theorem, we have $AB^2 = 8^2 + 15^2 = 289$, so

$$AB = \sqrt{289} = 17.$$

The sine of $\angle B$ is $\frac{8}{17}$. Applying the 'inverse sine' facility on a calculator gives the result $\angle B \simeq 28.1°$. Then the remaining angle is given by $\angle A = 90° - \angle B \simeq 61.9°$.

Solution 4.1

(a) The line passes through $(x_1, y_1) = (5, -2)$ and $(x_2, y_2) = (7, 4)$. Hence the parametric equation expressions $x = x_1 + t(x_2 - x_1)$ and $y = y_1 + t(y_2 - y_1)$ lead to

$$x = 2t + 5, \quad y = 6t - 2.$$

(b) If $x = 2t + 5$, then $t = \frac{1}{2}(x - 5)$. Hence we have

$$y = 6t - 2 = 6 \times \tfrac{1}{2}(x - 5) - 2 = 3x - 17;$$

that is, the equation of the line is

$$y = 3x - 17.$$

(c) If $x = 5$, then $y = 3 \times 5 - 17 = -2$. If $x = 7$, then $y = 3 \times 7 - 17 = 4$. Hence both $(5, -2)$ and $(7, 4)$ satisfy the equation found in part (b).

Solution 4.2

(a) The line segment joining (x_1, y_1) and (x_2, y_2) can be parametrised as

$$x = x_1 + t(x_2 - x_1), \quad y = y_1 + t(y_2 - y_1),$$

with t in the range $0 \leq t \leq 1$ (see the end of Subsection 4.1). Here $(x_1, y_1) = (-2, 4)$ and $(x_2, y_2) = (3, 1)$, so the parametrisation is

$$x = 5t - 2, \quad y = -3t + 4 \quad (0 \leq t \leq 1).$$

(b) The semi-circle has centre $(a, b) = (1, 1)$ and radius $r = \sqrt{2}$. Putting also $k = 1$ in the general equations

$$x = a + r\cos(kt), \quad y = b + r\sin(kt),$$

we obtain the parametric equations

$$x = 1 + \sqrt{2}\cos t, \quad y = 1 + \sqrt{2}\sin t.$$

In order to describe the semi-circle shown, an appropriate range for t is $-\frac{3}{4}\pi \leq t \leq \frac{1}{4}\pi$, since the angle between the diameter and the positive x-axis is $\frac{1}{4}\pi$. (Another suitable range is $\frac{5}{4}\pi \leq t \leq \frac{9}{4}\pi$.)

Index